Beauty In My Bones

Honoring the Women of My Family Clan

Beauty In My Bones

Honoring the Women of My Family Clan

Robin White

Foreword by Terrence J. Roberts Ph.D.

Member of Little Rock Nine

Copyright

Printed in the United States of America

First Printing, 2020

ISBN: 978-1-951883-02-7

Butterfly Typeface Publishing

PO Box 56193

Little Rock AR 7215

For Yaya

... who often told me that I have a divine purpose, and when unwarranted challenges were to befall me, it is incumbent to live on purpose, and to accept and see others in their evolution. Yaya taught me to take time to know and understand thyself and lean into my own understanding while flourishing on goodness and ingesting life lessons and the sweetness of integrity.

She left me deep-rooted in a tapestry of pride.

The Family Moral Compass

The family main vein is born out of the ordinariness of divinity, a secured realm to garner transformation in our sanctuary, the Kitchen in Barbara Ree's place, in which emotional disclosure is applied as a tool encouraging camaraderie with a vein of truth peppered with multiple spiced stories, rhymes of laughter and tears flowing with a timeline of love in action simmering in every meal recalibrating, readjusting, reflecting, restricting, and restoring over spans of betrayal, insecure-ness, sickness, and manipulation only to find a silver lining of comfort bonded in the concept of family, marinated in humanity, wrapped around the spirit of a people-centered on food and the core of the home, our Kitchen!
It is the family's staple and the cornerstone of every family gathering.

Table of Contents

Foreword

Robin White has chosen to shower us with grace to cover us in the love she first knew from her Yaya. Her autobiographical monograph is the vehicle through which she has chosen to share her rich memories of a life filled with a scintillating continuum of the best to humanity's worst. Out of this cornucopia of experience has come a woman filled to overflowing with love for self, for others, for life itself. And, best yet, she has invited us to share the life experience's bounty as she has lived it. "To what end," you may ask? And well, you should! Why should anyone else be interested in the life story of any other individual?

The answer is found in the realization that this drama we call life is a relational enterprise. We need each other. Absent a viable umbilical cord, we have no beginning. Once that lifeline is severed, we find ourselves ever in search of connectors that will bind us to those to whom we are drawn as if by some invisible thread. Whether kinfolk, fictive kin, significant or insignificant others, all have a claim on our bodies, minds, and souls.

Robin White opens wide the windows into her life in this honest outpouring of thoughts, memories, emotions, and poetic musings. In so doing, she teaches us about the value of relational integrity, the glue that cements the bond between people who long to love each other even if the pain of that love is too great to bear. Robin's story is unique, but the elements are not. All who read these lines will know variations of the themes she weaves throughout her narrative. It has been said that true poets craft words that allow readers to feel their own and not the poet's emotional center. Beauty In My Bones takes you directly to that place where you can laugh, all of your laughter, and cry, all of your tears.

Without reservation, I invite you to read this book to experience the power of one who believed from the start that none of the hurdles placed in her path would be too much to overcome. As you bear witness to her winding trek through the uneven terrain of America vitiated by a virulent strain of racist ideology and compounded by the willful ignorance of putative Christians, you are privileged to see possibilities for self and others.

Through this vision of her life's journey, Robin White invites you to consider digging down into your own center to find the core reasons you face each day and welcome any and all of the challenges that meet you at daybreak on any and every given day.

Respectfully submitted,

Terrence J. Roberts, PhD

Preface

Wounded Wombs

I was supposed to complete my manuscript in June, not fully understanding why, I stopped writing to mourn the world, sitting in low-grade depression, unable to wrap my mind around all those souls gone, taken from their loved ones–not realizing that I would soon mourn the loss of another loved one.

Not concerned about what society may think of me, but more concerned about family, and yet, so many of them assured me they loved and trusted me, and my narrative is my own. They have watched me from my girlchild days come unto my being to claim my essence. However, it was not until August 18, as we buried my dear sister, my comrade and one of the three girlchild conspirators MaeMae that I slowly began to understand the unspoken message. It seems a piece of me has been leaving since losing Versie, Clemmie, MaryAnn, and now MaeMae.

It was at Mae Mae's repast, while consumed with life and reflectively looking at over one hundred fifty family members and friends, silently witnessing the next generation, I was pleased standing next to Pookie and Lil June, realizing that when we leave, our families will be alright.

My family is female dominated; we are an extension of eight generations. I dutifully noted our ancestries, as we are born from wounded wombs, the origins of our generational trauma. Even so, we are not junk; we hail from strong roots scattered all over the South transported across the transatlantic. I sit and listen to the lilt in their voices, their truths, sighs of defeats laced with purpose and determination.

It is imperative to pay tribute to the women in our family, even those with complex lives, who continues to stand with the strength to embrace, love, and teach through all their pain. A lesson I learned from my former generations is that a warrior peacefully walks through the chaos and recognizes the reckoning with an accelerated need to stand in their convictions, inspiring others to stand in their shine.

They taught me to celebrate my global sisters encourage them to move gracefully with a spiritual consciousness when faced with disturbing times and unforgiving days. It is hope that dwells within me, even with a heavy heart I stand, and never back down to overcome such soul injuries.

All women, especially women of color, sometimes seek coverage in an ounce of humanity. From the love of family, I come in from the cold immersed in the folds of their warmth; although we stand at the intersection of diverse paths, it is their love that lets me know that I am not a bad person, from the wounded womb comes a daughter of the universe. I encourage all my sisters to self-validate; you need no permission for your existence. Abandon the shadows to no longer live in the space of occupancy apology: consistently apologizing for your intelligence, faith, and the color of your skin.

You are remarkable and deserve to know the value of love, not the fictional fairy tales, but the weight of true raw love in all its pain and glory. Live in the now, lean into the new, and stand in your shine to love conditionally. I don't believe in unconditional love. When one is abused for a period of time, their rhythm changes, and the relationship becomes conditional. If you don't love and protect yourself, then who will? Be unapologetically you. Pain doesn't discriminate; it is incumbent upon you to marinate into the comfort of your being for self-discovery and color yourself with love.

It was watching Sparkle, Angel, Angie, Nikki, Nova, Alexis, Whitney, Quita, and Coco that gave me the courage to step into this journey. The women in my family needs to know that despite what come their way; they will face it head on knowing that there is *Beauty In Their Bones*!

I am so proud of whence I hail because family is absolute!

Robin White

Acknowledgments

I must give props to the Creator, for He loved me so much, that He chose my Yaya (mother) as a vessel for me to come through, which leaves me most grateful. Although our ways parted in the physical form when I was age eleven, the legacy she left for me to maintain is strong. I am very fortunate to have come through her as she calared (colored) me with love.

My Yaya taught me to observe, be still, and hear. As I was often placed in a position to grow, I learned to trust at face value, through the eyes and heart of a child. I was taught to live with a divine purpose, and when faced with unwarranted challenges, to openly demonstrate how to live on purpose and in the face of fear and make every effort to see others in their own evolution. She taught me to know thyself, and lean into my own understanding, while flourishing on goodness and ingesting the sweetness of integrity.

She left me deep rooted in a tapestry of integrity, conditional love, and purpose with the capacity to endure life's baffling cyclones of change. She left me with the will to nurture, cultivate and grow from inner self.

I recall the command of her walk, infectious dimpled smile, the slight turn of her head, and the strength of her back as she held her head so high. Her lengthy hair easily transformed into a French bun, her signature hair style. Her slim fingers lovingly touched mine as she patiently taught me to make hot water cornbread, brown stew chicken, greens and our traditional family caramel cake.

Yaya, if you can hear me, these thoughts are just for you:

She has been removed as my heart aches for more.
She interchanges like a shadow behind closed doors.
I'm reminded of her scent;
my mind is cloudy as the wind shifts
and blows her memories around.
It is because of her, I fearlessly stand,
yet she can't be found.

Often, I wonder, why did it happen, when I was a long distance away?
When Jah came a calling my Yaya that day.
In all my grief, I can understand why
Jah wanted a person like her,
poised with dignity and so confident and sure.

I love her like no other and to me she will always be,
my world navigator, and lifelong educator;
with love she calared me.
She was my one true friend
during my girlchild crisis,
when I thought my world would end.

She gifted me the love of life,
the joy of spice,
when I couldn't make the grade;
she set wisdom in my shade
and empowered me
underneath the Church tree.
She calared me with love.

M. J. although you have gone on, I am grateful for our time together in Albuquerque. You were constantly empowering me, in recognizing my spirit. You saw me and accepted me with all my faults and baggage. You pointed out my writing style while we were securing grant funding for our youth programs. You told me that there was a fire burning inside me and I am not going to be able to contain it hiding from my true calling. I want you to know that I heard you and I am working on it.

Lisa C., you constantly pushed me and even went so far to reach out to Oprah Winfrey's people. I thought, how can I continue to keep my head down when you are willing to go all out. Well, I have stepped out on all of our faith and am grateful that you fought for me when I was afraid for many reasons, and today, there are none. I can only move forth and stand in my convictions sharing my narratives.

Introduction
My Reflection

I am a product of those who reared me, imbued in wisdom, filled with moral courage, social integrity, and the will to survive and thrive.

As a *girlchild*, I experienced multiple teachings while moving from house to house as a suitcase kid. By all accounts, traditional school was not a priority. Yet, I received an education as my elders enlisted pragmatic methods to develop my mind, body, and spirit.

In my circle of teachings, many had their hands on me as I learned about universal justice and love through a child's eyes.

Many times, my mirrored reflection failed to acknowledge me with a smile. This dark-skinned woman with almond shaped eyes, expansive nose, and soup cooler lips was confined to low self-esteem and the belief of being undeserving of all that is good. But that was when I was a *girlchild*.

I'd reflect *'pon* (upon) *Yaya* (mama), revisiting the few short years we had together, an eyewitness to a dynasty of self-validation. A short time of her teachings that nurtured and cultivated my soul instilled in me service ideology, community consciousness, and a profound love for humanity. She planted a seed that stirs my soul for humanity and community.

Constantly evolving, and as society's teachings set in, shaping and molding me, without failure my false sense of confidence was shaken.

How do you unlearn the learned? How do you attain the courage to reject society's distorted conditioning that devalues your experiences?

Truth be told, I dared to sit 'pon myself several years back, wrestled outward until all the knowing, the journey to recover the broken pieces of me, to stand and claim the inner most me surfaced from within.

Hear me this, the need to fortify my bloodline is astounding, and more empowering than any propaganda beset 'pon (upon) me. It is akin to the fierceness of a spirit's unrest and bolder than passion of a windstorm before a hurricane.

What role must I assume to leave my imprint on the world? How do I contribute to my lineage knowing the impact of lies and deception, the false justification weighed upon us?

They taught me, "There is beauty in my bones!"

My family clan is female dominated and the life legacy of our blood line is chosen before birth. As ambassadors, we are born into a circle of family and friends, cultivated for our true destiny to stand in our truth vein.

My bloodline would erroneously suffer if I spent lengthy periods of time as a *nega-holic,* marinating in self-victimization from society's prescription of self-hatred and bitterness. My journey through the habitation of my mind happens to exist because Yaya (mother) *calared* (colored) me *wif* (with) *lobe* (love).

The Family Moral Compass

My appreciation of food began early on. My Yaya was not only the family's core, but the pillar of my life as I watched her through a child's eyes create some of the greatest dishes from the kitchen of the poor.

The kitchen was the family gathering place for small talks, or a caucus when we were plotting who-knows-what.

Most importantly, family was always around, and it was our sanctuary, our place of security, no matter the threat from bad weather, crazy family members, neighbors, or insecure times.

Yaya made everything from scratch. From Hog Head Cheese or Souse to the family's traditional Carmel Cake or Pineapple Upside Down Cake and Banana Puddin' (which I taught my sons while they were in High School).

However, my weakness to a fault was when Yaya would make candied Yams or Sweet Potato Pon. I more than likely was going to get into trouble if the food of the day had anything to do with sweet potatoes. Sometimes, Yaya would send me to spend the night with family or friends just to protect me from myself. There was something about the combination of nutmeg, vanilla flavor, and butter mixed in batter that was intoxicating. The mixture just did something to my heart, made me feel good and for some unexplainable reason, it all belonged to me. My siblings said I suffered a short circuit.

I could tell you exactly what was on the stove, whether it was shrimp and grits, fried catfish, or buffalo. Dirty rice smelled sharper than red beans and rice, and plain virgin rice had this aroma that smelled clean and so inviting.

I watched Yaya eat baking powder six years for her bad heart; this was my mother's way of self-medicating for her heart condition.

However, the prescription she provided for my heart at age seven with *conditional* love are a significant part of my being today. (You love unconditionally until forced to do otherwise often due to betrayal). She had me stand on the large flour can, set the ingredients for a pound cake before me, and with careful precision, I went to work in creating my first pound cake from scratch under Yaya's loving care.

It was in those sentimental moments that I learned about my Grandyaya Zelda, my Great twin Uncles, Amos and Amis of Native American and Creole heritage, Uncle Buddy, and cousin Bright Eyes.

My GrandBaba (male elder) often passed in the white world because he was very light skinned, with a fine grade of hair and green eyes. His sisters, T.T. Bertha, Minnie, and Mary were just as fortunate, but they chose not to. All my cousins called Yaya "Auntie Barbara Ree." They speak of her with admiration. I know it was not just because she was light skinned and looked white. I know it was because she had a good heart and loved her family.

I can still feel her gentle touch on small hands as she covered mine and patiently taught me to make Johnny Cakes. However, because there were so many men and women in the family named Johnny or Johnni who claimed the cakes were named after them, we started calling them Flap Jacks.

Today, I have the ability to make anything from scratch. Cooking is therapeutic, and it provided time for me and Yaya to be joined in the kitchen creating recipes from the heart.

I lost Yaya at age eleven, but she left me deep-rooted in her love for spices, cooking, and making magic in the kitchen entwined with strong family values. The recipes from her heart became prescription for mine.

When I create a meal, the second thing people say (after "this is so good") is, "What is this called?"

I earnestly reply, "I don't know."

It's just something I made up, and no, I never write down the recipe, because it's in my head and heart. I genuinely feel it.

Turmeric potatoes, or shrimp tacos with five Chinese spices and ginger sugar, sage chicken, and vegetarian pasta with ginger are just a few of the creations that came alive in my kitchen.

In the wake of Katrina, I was compelled to gather recipes from family and friends as my grandchildren reminded me how important it is to write them down. Thus, I began to write *Recipes from La Nouvelle Orleans,* a cookbook inspired by Yaya.

It's funny; I enjoy making the dishes more so than eating them.

Yaya had very little, yet she had the capacity to create meals that provided us comfort, love, and a sense of security. Nothing is more rewarding than a soulful meal from the heart.

The House on Adams Street
The Border

In the beginning, when we lived on 13th Adams in the early sixties, this area was called The Border. It butted up against Broadway, which was the main vein through Gary, IN and separated neighborhoods.

My eldest sister, Gertrude, was in charge of us while Yaya worked as a nanny in Chicago, Illinois. She reported to work Sunday evening and returned to us early Fridays.

There were eight of us and now seven, my sister Lizbeth crossed over at age 19. Her last visit to Mississippi proved to be fatal as she returned sickly. The family legend is that ole' man Judd was infatuated with her. Hell, she was only fourteen at the time, how in the world can an ole man be fascinated with a girlchild? Well, she didn't take to him as he hoped, and the whispers are that he fixed her.

I enjoyed the Adams House.

Gertrude was the oldest; she had one green eye and one brown eye. She lost her green eye during one of those times she felt the need to jump Yaya.

Gertrude was the result of a physical violation between Yaya and one of the McMillen boys. In layman's term, Yaya was raped. In those days, men were men. Many gave witness to their quiet reserved mannerism as they silently denied the oppressive yokes as they raised the children that were the rape of their wives, sisters, aunts, and daughters.

My parents were Sharecroppers, as were all my aunts, uncles, and our grandparents. Multiple families lived on the McMillen and Augusta James Plantations.

Hear me this, Baba loved Gertrude just the same, perhaps even more than the rest of us. She was troubled from the start. *She didn't want good fine white folk's hair.* She had an undeniable mean spirit. She was pretty, though, and plenty of boys flocked around her. But they liked Lizbeth even more. Lizbeth was also light skinned like Yaya, although Gertrude's skin tone was lighter than theirs. Gertrude was shapely and really petite, her European features prominent. Lizbeth was also shapely, bow legged, pigeon-toed like Yaya, had big pretty eyes, and had a personality to mach. You were instantly drawn to her. It was her dimpled smile, quiet sprit, and happy eyes that made you feel welcomed.

We lived on 13th Adams from 1963-1965. My *girlchild* days were eventful, and when Yaya came home on the weekends, it seemed all the kids in the neighborhood looked forward to seeing her. They always whispered to me as if afraid to say it out loud. "Your mother is beautiful. How come some of you have long hair like your mother and some of you don't?"

"I don't know," I said, suddenly realizing the difference. I was one of the lucky ones with long hair. "And how come your hair is the color of clay dirt?" one of the kids snickered.

I was the lucky one with long hair, but also unlucky because it was red. And when the sun decided to bath in my hair the red was undeniable.

These were my neighborhood friends. We played Captain May I, the Devil and the Pie, Marbles, and we pitched pennies.

Although I didn't attend the same school as my neighborhood friends, we all started off together walking in the same direction and my school was the first stop. Upon entering a gated yard, I had to walk a few feet to the brown building shaped liked a steeple. As I descended the basement stairs to the main entrance, I held my breath. This was the dreaded longest walk.

All my classmates were girls and they dressed better than me. I had rough, thick hair and the girls with nice, wavy hair in ponytails, instead of French braids with barrettes or fresh bows, always reminded me of our hair difference.

Actually, they all looked like the teacher Ms. Brown, light skinned with straight teeth and good hair, except they didn't have a lot of moles on their face like she did. My punishments were at least three to four times daily. I had to stand in the corner, sit by myself, or not talk at the roundtable as others conversed. There was a small kitchen area where we received our snacks and lunches. For a child to bring their own lunch was unthinkable. In their eyes, my family was poor, backwards-thinking, country folks.

However, the girls fought over me to be on their sports or vocabulary activities. It was no wonder I hated school early on, even before first grade. My sister, Loretta, still teases me about that to this day. My hand still stings from us thinking about being popped with the ruler. Ms. Brown hit my little black hand like someone was slapping a mosquito. She told me, "Only big girls could take those licks without complaining or crying." Needless to say, being a big girl was more important than complaining to anyone at home.

Sometimes Ms. Brown directed me to silently read in the corner with my back to the class. She didn't know that reading was one of my favorite activities. I was reading way before I was five.

My world collapsed and my little body was filled with so much pain realizing she really didn't like me when she called me a "nappy headed geechie" through clenched teeth, almost as if she hated saying the word. It didn't' matter what I did, how smart I was, or even when I stopped speaking up for myself all together.

People think you don't remember things because you were young. But folks, children, babies, and teenagers have good memories. We just choose to store bad memories someplace outside of us because of the pain, the person, or the event that hurts us.

Sometimes, my neighborhood friends would wait for me outside the school gate so we could walk home together. We were pint sized kids that always expressed ourselves There were two fifth graders in the crew that felt responsible for the younger ones. We talked about everything and everyone was related to someone else in the group. They informed my siblings of the inappropriate behavior they witnessed before and after school on my behalf.

Lizbeth nodded and listened, my brother Johnny said he would come up to the school and whip them with his belt, and Gertrude said she would come up to the school and jump the teacher.

Lizbeth decided to walk with me and my friends to school. She witnessed my anxiety and took pity *pon* (upon) me. We ditched school and sat on the Froebel High School Lawn (the school Lizbeth attended). She entertained me all day.

We shared our problems at school and Lizbeth pushed me to come up with solutions regarding how I can make things better. My critical and analytical thinking and proactive skills were borne early on. After problem solving, we had sister time. Sister time is usually reserved for Saturdays, when all the female sibling, cousins etc. have to groom each other, which consist of washing and styling each other's hair.

Our sister time was so much fun. We laughed and ran around on the school grounds. I laid my head in her lap while she read to me. Lizbeth always talked to me as if I were a big person. To this day, I can't recall the name of the school, but everything else is vivid. The next year, the pain lingered as I walked past the school with my neighborhood friends going to Norton Elementary School.

Pon completion of homework and daily chores, we met outside to play. I looked forward to this until Yaya returned, and for some reason troubled managed to find me, guaranteeing a punishment that included me being stuck in the house. This was fine with me, because my desire to be around Yaya was strong.

We didn't have to converse. I had the capacity to self-entertain and clearly enjoyed the role as cooking assistant.

Yaya cut back on her nanny hours and was catering. She was busy working with other parents in the community and all they talked about was a change was coming. Yaya and Ms. Arlene spent a lot of time together on their off days and holidays. They were always planning events that involved the neighborhood children or the whole community.

However, this particular day was their special time together as they going to watch a television broadcast.

At home on Adams Street, our yard was nothing but hard dirt. On this particular November day, Yaya was in a hurry to pin line the clothes. They were going to be stiff as boards, but she swore the natural air made the clothes smell fresh and kept the colors longer.

All the young ones were downstairs at Ms. Ada's watching cartoons with Jack and Niel and my older siblings were out and about. I don't recall Gertrude ever going to school. Yaya was rushing to watch a special program on television. I was sitting and digging in the hard dirt, when suddenly our neighbor's dog started whining, barking, and then howling. It frightened me a wee bit because King didn't fuss much.

Suddenly, Ms. Arlene came running through the yard screaming, "They shot him. They killed our John. Baby, President Kennedy is gone!" She was bent over with her hands on her knees then to her heart, she was just shaking her head and twisting her hands in her apron and said, "Baby, President Kennedy is gone!"

Not quite understanding, my body slowly turned to watch Yaya's reaction to this bad news. She then screamed, fell to her knees, and King howled louder, the basket tumbled over and the clothes lay in the dirt. The piercing scream hit my ears. It seemed time stood still and to this day, I don't know when I reached her.

I had never seen Yaya so distraught and this scared me. Crying with her, clinging to her with my little cold, dirty hands, I attempted to wipe her tears away. It was the men in the community who came to our rescue. They picked Yaya up like she was a baby and carried her up the long flight of stairs.

They laid Yaya on the couch and tried to get her to drink some water. Someone called Dr. Mitchell and demanded that he get over to the house. I stepped back watching the outpour of love for Yaya, and I was thinking Yaya is important, they love her.

Suddenly, her hysteria stopped, and she went silent. This concerned the men even more. They could respond to hysteria, but they didn't know what to do with silence.

I was twelve before I began to fully understand what the Kennedys meant to the Black community. Yaya love John Kennedy, but Senator Robert Kennedy had a special place in Yaya's heart. She strongly believed if he became President, she would receive the adequate medical care for her heart condition and things would improve for us.

Yaya, who had a gentle, yet demanding spirit, a piece of her also died that day. She was quieter and withdrawn. Her community activities slowed down. Eventually, she returned to her nanny job full time and we fell into our old routine.

I could tell Yaya was restless when she was home on the weekends and in less than a year in November of 1965, we moved to 15th and Massachusetts.

Hankering

Comforting sheets provide refuge

Astounding inaudible cries breaking boundaries

Lips part to emancipate what's inside

A breakthrough for the real liberation

Cautioning a sensation beyond recreation

Of course, things are different now

Breakthrough

I learned to embrace the gypsy flowing through Yaya as a child.

We migrated from Louisiana, Mississippi, and South Carolina, to Chicago, Indiana, Detroit, and only to return to Indiana.

At age six, my world was filled with wonder.

We are cultivated for our true destiny and often faltering under the enormity of existing.

At times, I was safely settled with the neighborhood Yayas who had a say in my nurturing. Yayas are women, not necessarily mothers, just older than me. They could be cousins, neighbors, or great aunts, who naturally provide direction for the children. We dared not disrespect our Yayas without severe consequences.

No matter where we lived, I always went back through memories to that place called, "The Border."

It was strongly family occupied. There were lots of kids running around playing tag, one-two-three-four-red light-green light, captain may I, cricket, the devil and the pie, and many other games we invented to amuse ourselves.

Even though some bad seeds were beginning to breach our harm free environment, disturbing our innocence, we were still carefree living on The Border.

As I reminisce, my mind strolled through the apartment on 13th and Adams that wrapped love around eight children and an adult.

I traveled up the stairs two at a time: 2,4,6,8,10. *Whew*, pause to breathe and then sing: 12, 14, 16, 18, 20. Reaching the door, and turning the knob, because the door was hardly ever locked.

A wonderful aroma welcomed me. Aint anything like coming home to brown stew chicken, dirty rice, Johnny Cakes, and candied yams. Yea, I'd arrived!

The kitchen table, named Maelee, was my favorite piece of furniture. Maelee looked like she was fit for a family of fifteen instead of nine. She sat upright, as if royalty, leg bowed with knobbed feet, ready to run anytime.

Sitting under Maelee and watching friends and family was my favorite past time. Maelee was the center of everything - absorbing everybody's secrets. You see, I was often punished for doing crazy shit. Therefore, my only form of entertainment was the dining table and eyewitness to the neighborhood action.

I'd dress Maelee up with fancy cloth, lay under her, and share my girlchild troubles. Maelee was a fitting name, because everybody in the family was named Mae or Lee.

Maelee let me know that *everything gonna be aw'right* with her strong presence. She taught me to be still, listen to the noise, and gain a deep appreciation for the silence too.

The looking glass was in the family room and I could see the Corner Store.

Everybody said the owner was nice, because he was a Jew.

All I saw was a round Buckra (White person) who would pat us on the head and backside all the time. I thought a Jew was somebody that treats black kids like they matter. When we ran through the store talking loud, Mr. Michael didn't holler at or threaten us, he just talked to us and, most importantly, listened to our replies. Mr. Michael didn't tell us to shut up. He gave several of us small responsibilities, such as emptying trash, sweeping certain areas of the store, and greeting our neighbors. In return, he gave us cash and talked to us about saving our money. I thought a Jew was somebody that let all the black kids work in his store.

The looking glass gave me eyewitness to the light skinned family across the street, with good hair and face dimples. The three sisters were always together holding hands. The oldest girl constantly wanted me to give my brother love messages.

He be right there, why don't she tell him herself?

In the middle of the block was Rita's Place, where you could find any of the older neighborhood kids, even my siblings. You could play music over the juke box and eat the best, greasiest burgers in town. Even better than King Kastle and Coney Island.

I loved to watch people dance and often joined in showing them the latest dances. I had no problem getting on the dance floor and dancing with myself. Mikey and Dino would sit outside and breathe in bags all day.

One day I'm goanna buy me some air to breathe in those paper bags.

A holler down the street was a huge girl named Baby Fruity. There wasn't a damn thing *fruity* about her, so I called her Baby Hughey. I thought people should move, she looked like she was gonna bust wide open with Hostess Hos Hos, Twinkies, chicken necks from Lee's Chicken Shack, and slabs of Ribs from Ray's Bar B Q. She waddled from side to side and snorted loudly. I don't think any store got drawers her size.

How her feet carry her big ole body?

Next door to us was a house filled with women.

I thought they were just a big ass family of girls. People called them "ladies of the night." We were warned by all the neighborhood Yayas "not to go near them 'no-good women', who were for sure going to hell."

It's amazing how you can look at folks and tell if they are going to hell. I guessed some of us got the hook up with God more so than others.

They looked like normal women to me in the daytime, but I never saw how they looked at night.

One day, I heard Yaya fussing at my sister Lizbeth for being around those fast women and how lucky she was to be in God's grace. One of those unfortunate women was found murdered in a hallway.

God, who wants to hurt those ladies? All they do is smile at you and wear funny clothes.

They called that area "The Border."

Buckras don't know everything. Aint nothing boring about this place. Something always happened on either corner.

Why come every time a police car turns the corner everybody runs?

You learn to run from the police early on, and it doesn't matter if you a girl or boy.

Folks got it all wrong, there is nothing boring about The Border.

Wrinkles In My Forehead

Every Saturday, the women in the family groomed each other. It became a practice to see which sister would take me on to wash and comb my hair. It was not until years later that I realized we were socializing, grooming, and bonding, even though I made it a challenging, unwanted chore.

At the first opportunity, I would run out the door with my hair flying in every direction. Family members and neighbors chased me down the street.

Once captured and returned to the torture chamber and Loretta or Gertrude would vice lock their legs around me and hold me down until my hair was braided.

Lizbeth always held my hand, talked to me, and gave me sweets during the torture.

They soon came up with the idea to strip me down to my T-shirt and undies at grooming time. Saturday morning rolled around, and I was disengaged from my clothes, but that didn't stop me from breaking for the door and running down the street with family members and neighbors in pursuit.

I was in the third grade, very small, and fast on my feet, but there was always somebody faster. There was no game plan, no hiding place to provide security, I just ran as long as my body would move.

T.T. Lucille, a friend of Yaya, had a sit-down talk with me. She schooled me on the significance of being a woman and how my sisters were charged with the heavy duty of preparing me for womanhood. She told me that if I kept giving the neighbors something to talk about, my behavior will bring dishonor to the family. T.T. Lucille talked Yaya into letting her press my hair. After two weekends of her burning my ears and me walking around with straightening comb burns on my ears, neck, and forehead, I was glad to get my hair washed and braided.

My childhood days were filled with fun memories because people were always around.

We lived in a village and everybody knew what clan or tribe to which you belonged.

I was knee high to a duck's ass and dark skinned with a crazy red hair color, especially when the sun hit it. It wasn't a pretty sight, and everybody teased me. My nickname was Red. My oldest son, my nephew, and my male cousin all have red hair. There were very few female red heads in the family.

Hanging out around shoeshine boxes became part of my past time so that I could swipe Black Shoe Polish. The elders would just watch me and didn't say anything to my parents or other family members. They figured that sooner or later, my little secret would be revealed. 'Pon deciding I had enough shoe polish to do the job, I started packing it in my thick hair, sitting in the bathroom looking in the mirror and putting it in like a perm, like my sisters did to their hair.

No one could tell me anything when I strutted out to the backyard to announce that my hair was now black. Everybody froze from shock; it seemed like forever passed before all hell broke loose.

Gertrude snatched me up and screamed, "What the hell did you do to your hair?"

"I dyed it black with shoe polish," I said, still unsure what the ruckus was about.

My sister Lizbeth grabbed me from Gertrude and was laughing so hard she was crying.

Loretta, Cousin Jimmy, and Aunt Wilma Mae were hysterical.

My heart was crushed because this was so important to me. I stood there, head bowed, and shame faced.

Upon further interrogation from Gertrude, it was revealed that I was swiping the shoe polish from the elders. They marched me right down the street to apologize and find out how much I owed. The elders saw me coming and declared that witnessing the sight of me walking down the street with Shoe Polish packed in my thick hair was worth the wait. They felt this incident was enough compensation and a story for life, so the shoe polish was on the house.

Gertrude made me sit on the front stoop so that the whole neighborhood could see me. I was sitting there, frowning in the hot ass sun thinking how I was going to kick her ass when I grew up.

As the sun pressed down on me, the shoe polish began melting and slide downs my neck. It was funky.

When Yaya returned home, my siblings were directed to hose me down. There was no protesting on my part. For the first time in my life, I welcomed a shampoo and fully cooperated.

Needless to say, Yaya jacked up my backside, not because of what I did to my hair, but because I stole.

Baba couldn't save me on this one, because too many people knew about it.

If they were charging a "stupid tax" in our household when I was growing up, my Yaya would've been rich.

I always got myself in a pickle acting out, doing and saying things before thinking about them.

A wrinkled forehead was a clear sign of trouble, according to Yaya and my siblings. Generally, the rule was I had to stay close to home and everybody had to keep a watchful eye on me. She'd check my forehead for wrinkles to see if I was going to have a good day or if someone else was going to have a bad day.

It's interesting, because growing up, I worked purposely to get rid of that idiosyncrasy. It transformed into an unconscious habit that everybody was aware of but me.

When I bat my eyes slowly, that meant that I was struggling to maintain my composure. However, if I bat my eyes rapidly, it meant that I didn't give a damn and somebody was about to get a

Sippianna ass whopping. *(A Sippianna ass whooping was me reaching way back to Mississippi and Louisiana, twirl like the rain through the Carolinas on into Indiana – a storm filled with a fearless wrath and inconsiderate to anything or anyone in the way.)* I would just run into you like a storm and be all over you, regardless your weight or height. To put it plain, I would reach back and knock you out!

Candied Yams

We lived on 15th and Massachusetts at the end of 1965 in Gary, Indiana. I should've seen it coming. Yaya had no problem with moving on or trying to make things better for whomever. We had already moved a lot and lived in several states before I was eight. I couldn't adjust to Detroit nor Lansing Michigan or New York, but Chicago, Illinois and Michigan City and Gary, IN suited me well. I didn't feel off balance as a child.

It seemed like Yaya got stronger and weaker at the same time, but she didn't let much get in her way. This is what I personally witnessed as a child. It sure taught me a lot.

Some people are addicted to chocolate, men, food, sex, or shopping. My addiction is sweet potatoes. I have a love affair with sweet potatoes. As a kid, I even preferred to eat sweet potatoes than go trick or treating! Candy didn't do it for me. It just wasn't satisfying - but Yaya's candied yams rocked.

Like most addictions, it has caused some serious trouble more times than not. My backside would take a whipping with ease if I knew that candied yams were my reward.

As poor as we were, the holidays were always special. I watched and assisted Yaya begin preparing for the holiday months in advance. She would make Fruit Cake from Scratch, preserving the fruit for months in Cherry Wine.

The Holidays were always good, there was always lots of food, the short bread Xmas Cookies with the pecans and powdered sugar, bowls of Pecans, Walnuts, and the Brazilian Nuts, along with Oranges and Apples.

It was Christmas Eve, and as I was walking through the kitchen singing and bouncing to Motown Xmas music, I lost my breath as my heart stopped and there on the table was a bowl of sweet potatoes batter ready to be laid in the pie crust. The pie crust was sitting on the stove. I can honestly say that my mind went blank. Moments later, cramped in the bottom of the kitchen cabinet, my face in the bowl as my lap held it. Soon here was commotion in the kitchen, cabinet doors were loudly opened as they banged against each other and slammed shut as if someone was in search of something.

Unfortunately, I paid it no never mind and continued to greedily consume the Sweet Potato batter. A light was creeping in, but my face was in the bowl inhaling the content. I was making all kind of inhuman sounds. The door was flung open and Yaya screamed from shock, everyone ran into the kitchen and there was a gale of laughter. My siblings were on the floor, the table, and falling up against the wall in laughter fits. I was straight up busted with sweet potato batter in my hair, ear, nose, and all on my clothes.

With this anxious look, I didn't know what to say, or how to feel, all I know is that Yaya should not have left the Sweet Potato batter around like that. It was so good, and I wasn't quite finished, my mind kept wandering back to the remaining batter. I know that was soul selfish, but rarely did I get in trouble, and most times others always came before me, except when it came to sweet potatoes.

Lizbeth helped unfold me from the cubbyhole, but I wasn't quite ready to give up the batter when Gertrude snatched it from my grasp. I was so outdone with her. I just wanted to bite her.

Yaya slowly shook her head and said, "I knew I should've sent you out, but I thought you would at least behave yourself tonight, with all the company over to keep you occupied."

I lowered my head and said, "I'm sorry." I tried to look sorry, but before I knew it, I asked, "Can I have some more?"

"If this is your weakness," Yaya laughed, "I thank the Lawd."

Ever venomous, Gertrude was quickly pouring out the remaining batter and I wanted to scream. Loretta and Lizbeth attempted to clean me up. They had to wrestle with me to get the batter out of my hair, so they doubled team me.

Heat was steaming off me, thinking about Gertrude throwing perfectly good batter away. She could have let me eat some more. Perhaps this is why I began to cause mischief. As my older siblings were fixing the bed, I had the nerve to run through the sheets, turn flips in the bed, playing capoeira, encouraging my younger siblings and cousins to do the same.

We were playing so hard (ajenga, flipping, jumping in the air almost to the ceiling), that I had forgotten all about my early discretions. The next thing I knew, a strap came across my backside.

Yep, Yaya tore my backside down.

You think that stopped me from swiping sweet potatoes?

Nope!

Yaya started sending me on long errands or made sure I was spending the night elsewhere when sweet potatoes were on the menu.

I now realize that she was protecting me from myself. I was like a pit bull. She knew I would keep coming and not let go, slamming into the wall repeatedly, just running up a blind alley.

Yes, to his very day, sweet potatoes are my number one weakness, and quite frankly there is no shame here, because my love for sweet potatoes was heartfelt, and Yaya made everything with love.

The Lioness

My birthday is the beginning of March.

The old wives' tale has been voiced to me many times,

"Those born in the month of March come in like a lion and

go out like a lamb."

My life has been totally the opposite.

As I stand timid as a lamb, the lioness often surfaces.

People are often misinformed

by their first impression of me.

I'm misjudged, treated rudely because I'm quiet and am

more into learning,

observing my surrounding than being heard.

I speak when there is something to say and I'm as fierce

as a Lioness when need be.

Non-Verbal Communication

Our house was always filled with music.

Mae turned me on to Andy Williams, Dean Martin, The Beatles, Old Blue Eyes Frank Sinatra, Johnny Mathis, Harry Belafonte, and Nancy Wilson.

Of course, we had plenty of in-house music: calypso and carnival from New Orleans that nobody listened to but us. Gullah music had specific rhythms or claps that I was drawn to. We danced to Zydeco, Cajun and Brass Bands.

But that was our music, it was in-house, and it's still the same today.

My oldest brother, Johnny, was nicknamed James Brown II at an early age. He was in talent shows at Emerson, Froebel and West Side High Schools, and he performed at the local community centers and Gary, Indiana Memorial Auditorium. Johnny performed in the same places the Jackson Five performed; he was a celebrity in his own right. I watched girls swoon over my brother to give him messages and had them be background dancers for him in the talent shows.

Johnny was a good, fun brother. We never fought. He played tricks on me a lot, but I often curbed his mischievous behavior. I put some Ex-Lax in Hershey bar wrappings and left it in the freezer. As a giving person, there was no cause for my brother to suspect anything when I gave him some of my candy out of the freezer.

I sweetly informed him that he ate some Ex-Lax after he gobbled it down. He hit the ceiling and ran to tell Yaya. Everyone was teasing him because he was the greatest prankster. He eventually forgave me and I was the top family prankster for the moment.

Although we are four years apart, Johnny and I were very close. He turned me on to *James Brown*, *The Five Stair Steps*, *The Dells*, and *The Delfonics*. He shared his love for music with me, as we were often dancing partners at home and in the community. I really thought that was special for a big brother to share his passion with a younger sister.

Gertrude was hard to read, she was strange, charismatic, and soft spoken. In the beginning, you didn't realize how domineering she was until she had reeled you in. She was high maintenance, needed a lot of attention, had a petite, small frame, a large stature, light skin, one brown eye, one green eye, and fine grade of hair (what folks back in the day called "good hair"). She was the oldest sibling and damn trying at times. The young family members favored her because of her European features, but the elders didn't trust her and kept their distance. She was crazier than a Louisiana Bayou Cricket.

Growing up with a household filled with siblings, cousins, aunts and uncles, you witness history in the making. Gertrude was a history lesson in and of herself. Even as a child, I knew she was brilliant, but the basket was still empty.

She had this way about her in which she made her rounds to family members, somehow leaving them all mad at each other after her visit when they were usually laughing, singing, cooking, playing games, and just genuinely happy. This changed in the wake of Gertrude's presence among them.

I learned quickly as a child you just watch everything and listen to survive. Like a sponge, I absorbed everything to strengthen my survival skills.

I loved Gertrude dearly, but learned early on to listen to *everything* she said and decipher it to understand what she *really* meant. Even though I paid close attention, she managed to get me twice.

The first time, I was trying to get Yaya to buy me a dress that we couldn't afford. I was perhaps 9 going on 10 and should have known better.

Gertrude was *cracking* (talking) her teeth with me.

"Daddy is over in Michigan City with his African People," Gertrude began. "You over here looking just like him and his people. Yaya can't stand you because you look just like him. That's why she won't buy you that dress you want."

I looked skeptical, so she kept going.

"Haven't you noticed you're the darkest of the children and have the strongest African features and you're the ugliest of the bunch of us?"

Slowly, my resolve broke and I started to believe her.

"If you want to get Yaya's goat and make her pay attention to you, just run away. She's sure to buy you that dress then."

My dumb ass fell into the pity pot. My sister gave me a dollar to run away and I left.

I actually spent the night in the hallway of a classmate, but early morning I walked into my house. I saw the anguish on Yaya's face and then I knew the hurt and unnecessary deliberate pain I had caused her.

It hurts my heart to this day, but when Yaya looked up and saw me, she jumped from that chair and screamed my name. Yaya grabbed me, crying and holding onto me. After checking my limbs, Yaya placed her forehead on mine, looked into my eyes, and shook her head as if she knew.

That's what Gertrude failed to realize, Yaya and I communicated with each other without verbal communication, we just knew.

I never gave Gertrude the satisfaction of letting Yaya know that she had used me as a weapon to hurt her, but I think Yaya knew. She never wanted to talk about it. This was a day that I learned the depth of a mother's love.

Gertrude had a very strong personality and a beautiful voice right along with Aretha Franklin and Mahalia Jackson. She had a small following of friends, leader of the pack.

She was born March 16 and I on March 6. We are both Pisces but like night and day, almost ten years apart. Gertrude turned me on to *Gladys Knight, Donny Hathaway, The Temptations*, and *Smokey Robinson*. I listened to *Aretha Franklin,*

Diana Ross, *The Supremes*, *Marvin Gaye*, and *Do Wop* groups on my own.

The second time she got me was when Gertrude instigated a fight between me and Loretta. Loretta was at least 19 or 20 and I was all of 13.

We moved from 539 Broadway to Delany Housing Projects at 2260 Harrison, the housing projects were located across from Roosevelt High School and on the other side was where the Jackson Five lived.

It was a three-bedroom house with multiple families, this include Gertrude and her husband and their four children. My three brothers had a room and Gertrude placed her son in that room. This left one room for my youngest sister, my older sister Loretta who was 19 or 20, her daughter and my three nieces, and me, all of 12. Gertrude told me and Loretta we had to fight over the room and we actually went at it. Loretta grabbed her baby and walked out the house crying as I was standing at the door crying watching her and my niece leave. My heart was so pained I thought it would bust.

Gertrude slapped me for crying and told me and Peaches her girls would be in the room with us. I didn't quite understand what I participated in, there were four bunkbeds in the room, and we were all fairly small but Peaches and Loretta.

I asked God not to forgive me and to please look after my niece and sister. If this still hurts me, I know if Loretta reflects upon those days, it must pain her. This was the best thing Loretta did was to get away from the poison we were immersed in. I think Loretta had offended Gertrude in some manner and Gertrude decided that there couldn't be two women in the house and I was the tool used to get rid of her problem.

Family's Enemy Friend

Her eyes were fixed on finding Pokeweed

as she strolled down the dirt road.

She mentally noted

how her return caused such pandemonium.

The whispers, "you and the other are about the same age.

You could be twins alike, 'cept you have darker skin."

There was much confusion in their words of warning till

the day she happened 'pon the family's enemy friend.

There he rocked back and forth, older than olden,

skeletal hands beckon her near,

she froze as her eyes took in the family fear.

He looked like everyone's grandpapa or great grandpapa;

thin as a willow, the ancestor whispered beware chi,

for he is strong and fit.

So much family legend, no, he can't be the same,

the one they laid blame on fixing my sister

in her youthful years.

Unafraid and filled with rage their eyes locked,

and then she instantly knew that this was the man that

cursed her sister, Lois.

He called her by the name of the other.

The family's enemy friend stood half bent, tears flowing

as he sought forgiveness for his earthly sins.

She witnessed the name of the other fall from his lips

over and over again.

She then knew that Jah brought her to this place.

She was destined to meet the family's enemy friend.

She was the same age as the other, people testified that

they looked twins alike,

ole man Judd begged her for forgiveness,

not noting the darker skin.

Losing Lizbeth

Not long after the Corner House on 15th Mass., we moved to 222 West 11th Avenue, Gary, IN in 1966. I was enrolled in Norton school. I thanked God; I was back with the neighborhood friends.

Yaya cut back her hours because Lizbeth was really suffering; they didn't know what was wrong with her.

On her last trip from Mississippi, Lizbeth had returned sickly. The family legend was that old man Judd was fascinated with her. Hell, she was only fourteen then.

How in the world can an old man be fascinated with a child?

Well, she didn't take to him, and the whispers were that he fixed on her.

I remember walking to a convalescent home to visit my sister. She was nineteen years old. Five years was fast 'pon us and Yaya was struggling with Lizbeth's illness.

I was ten and can't rightfully recall which tragedy struck first.

The ambulance came to the house to collect Lizbeth and take her to the hospital. My older siblings, Gertrude, Loretta, and Johnny went to the hospital with Yaya.

I was lying in the bed with Peaches, Vincent, and JR. Then, Lizbeth was in the bed with us. She always sucked her two middle fingers and had a habit of folding your ears. She loved to play with our ears.

"When you grow up," Lizbeth said that night, "you are going to be responsible for the rest of the kids. If you mistreat them, I'll return and slap you so hard; my handprint will be left on your face."

I fell asleep in Lizbeth's arms.

I was awakened by heartfelt screams, crying and sniffling.

"What is everybody crying about," I asked as I walked into the kitchen.

"Lizbeth crossed over," they said to me.

"No, she's not," I protested. "She was in the bed with me."

They ran into the bedroom. Yaya stood looking at me.

"What did she say?" Yaya wanted to know. "Why did she visit you?"

This was no family mystery. I got visitors all the time.

I repeated what Lizbeth said.

In the same year, Yaya was getting her groove back and I now understood what she was doing.

I was ten and knew who Robert Kennedy was.

Yaya and the community were on fire.

It was déjà vu.

Yaya and I were in the hallway when our neighbor, Ms. Rosa, a huge woman, came running up the stairs. You could feel the stairs shake as if a rumble was going on.

She frantically screamed, "They shot Bobby. They shot Bobby! Oh my God."

The piercing scream matched the horror on Yaya's face and the terror in her eyes.

"No, no. Not again," Yaya mumbled as she turned and crawled up the steps.

Johnny was home.

He picked her up and Yaya shut herself off in her room.

She didn't go back to work for a while.

It was during this time when the family learned that Yaya had a bad heart condition.

There was eight of us, then just seven. Lizbeth crossed over at the age of nineteen, Yaya had to make the decision to take her off the breathing machine, the doctor said she was suffering too much. No parent wants to go before their child. This took a lot out of Yaya.

Then, Loretta and I began getting closer.

Loretta was becoming my inspiration. She always shared books with me; she could easily bribe me to do her chores with sweet potato turnovers and books. I somehow became a fixture of the living room near Yaya's room, with a book always nearby.

Invisible Life Lessons

I have many fond memories of sister companionship, including my own birthright sister, Loretta.

On weekends we groomed one another, we washed and combed each other's hair. They taught me to French braid at an early age.

In her youth, Loretta was pretty ambitious. She was going to Emerson High Night School and worked at Westville, Indiana State Mental Hospital. The big white bus used to pull up in front of our house on 11th Avenue to pick her up for work. The writing on the bus read, "Westville Mental Correctional Center."

It was a warm summer night as we exited Emerson School in Gary, IN off 7th Avenue. I was in the fifth grade and was proud to be with my older sister as she allowed me to attend night school with her now and then. We walked side by side, taking short cuts, and running through alleys. Back then, alleys were as wide as driveways, not small like they are today.

We were just sisters having fun, enjoying each other's company. We were so innocent, unmindful of our surroundings.

A car slowed down heading in the opposite direction as we neared the corner of Massachusetts.

We almost made it to Broadway Street on 11th Avenue without violation.

In my older years, I now know that Broadway Street was the dividing line, symbolic of the railroad tracks.

Our sister time was shattered as two white boys leaned out of the car and shouted, "Let's get those niggers."

They sounded so angry.

What had we done wrong to offend them?

It didn't take long for me to learn that my dark skin is a sin.

Our very existence offended certain groups of people.

However, this particular night, my temper got the better of me, and I yelled in my powerful girlchild voice at the boys, standing with my convincing bad attitude, as if that empowered me, "Leave us alone, we ain't done nothing to your dumb asses!"

I was downright furious; they were interrupting my sister time.

I don't quite recollect all the words that came out of my mouth, but my sister's shocked look sent chills through me. It occurred to me that maybe this was something I really couldn't handle.

Loretta was nearly dragging me. I was wrestling with her as the boys made a U-turn in the car. She was crying, pleading for me to run, and I was feeling sorry for her.

Her fear transferred to me. It was the same type of fear that set over the family, when Uncle Mel was murdered down in the Delta.

This is the worst type of fear beset 'pon you. In which you are rendered helpless.

'Pon realizing what could really happen to us, we turned and ran like track stars. The boys were throwing beer bottles out of the car. We could hear the bottle break against the buildings and felt the beer and small glass pieces hit our legs.

Shit. Loretta didn't have to say another word, I was keeping up with her.

Broadway is a busy section and the police station was two blocks down on 13th. It was 1968, I was ten years old, and knew that the police station was not a place of sanctuary. We galloped across Broadway as the boys were held up at the stop light. I told Loretta to follow me past Adam Street and turned down Washington. I sure didn't want them to see us enter our house at 222 West 11th Avenue.

However, it didn't take long for the assailants to catch up with us. I ran straight into the corner store. Neighbors heard the ruckus; some people were sitting out on their stoops. They saw us running from the threatening car. Neighbors exited their homes and the store to bring witness to what was happening. One neighbor threw an obstacle at the car, another began to shoot up in the air, and the men began to move around silently with weapons.

The car moved dangerously fast, speeding up the street. As they turned the corner, all we saw were backlights that resembled red blinking eyes laughing at us. Loretta and I were surrounded by love. We were safe at last as neighbors hugged us, swearing to protect us.

We thought that being in the North was different. We had been trespassing all along, and on this particular night, we just happened to get caught. It was a rude awakening for me, as I learned that your skin color and ethnicity determine what side of town you live on.

That was a frightening experience. At an early age, I learned that mine and the lives of others depends on knowing the *White Man's* rules. It didn't matter where you lived; the North and South were one and the same. The neighborhood was quiet, but loud with anticipation for nearly a month. Relatives and friends were on watch for what was to come from either the police or more mean white people.

I thank God that nobody ever came back to harass us. In good conscience, I would not be able to live it down if anyone were hurt because I forgot about such stupid rules.

That was my fifth-grade year. Every now and then when traveling in sundown through towns or when faced with unfamiliar territory, memories of that night return to me.

So much has changed in our lives, yet certain unspoken things remain the same. I am a bound continuum of growth from knowledge and my own ignorance.

Loretta, I'm so sorry that society has crippled your mind, stunting your growth. I'm sorry for the negative impact both the North and the South visited 'pon you.

Loretta lost her drive to live openly beyond confined walls, she exists with dried up ambitions in her own world. Loretta walks to the library with a wagon and returns home with a wagon filled of books, as she hides out in her room and reads, while the world turns.

Yaya had her way of dealing with grief and life disappointments. Once again, we moved and found true comrades. I loved the house on 11th avenue. I could scale the walls in the gangway to the roofs and sit up there to watch the world, the cars go by, and the multiple white people driving through our neighborhood to and from work. We lived there three years and in 1969 we moved to 539 Broadway above Toggery Store.

The apartments were huge, and our kitchen gave way to the roof. Oh, I loved the roof.

Oso Tunde

The Seer Comes Again

As a girlchild I received visitors rather I wanted to or not. Most times it happened before or while one was transitioning. Last year one of my granddaughters was laying on me and said "Gramgam you have ghost in this house," I replied no baby, they are not ghosts they are spirits."

Spirits have always been a part of me, and though the teachings of my elders I pay homage to them with very little effort because it comes naturally. Do you recall as a child visiting your elders and there were small saints around the house, or a glass of water on the table, and a bowl of frit you were not allowed to eat?

After a long absence during my adult years and returning to my chosen path, I was blessed with the name Oso Tunde---the seer comes again.

Some of my cousins refuse to spend the night with me after we attend a homegoing (funeral) because I generally get visitors.

Some of us pay closer attention to our gut instincts, conscious or intuitions. You can sense when someone is sad, or your body reacts in convulsions when you meet someone that is bad. Sometimes spirit whispers warnings and most time we choose to ignore. When we doubt the voice that guides we doubt ourselves.

As a child Oyo Rinde (joy walks in) was presented during my naming ceremony. It is now realizing that the given name was correct, in spite of life challenges, my greatest joy was self-discovery, learning the capacity to rely on my internal strength and socially and emotionally leaning into family and community values. My greatest lesson was no matter where the roads led I a child of the universe and part of destined communities.

We lived at 539 Broadway above Millers Toggery Store in a three-bedroom apartment. Loretta, our baby sister, Peaches, and I shared a bedroom. The apartment had large windowsills and I often would sit on them and people watch. We also made up stories about the people we watched. This was also the best spot for watching parades.

Johnny was sitting in the kitchen near the back door on the phone, as usual lying to some girl. I was sitting in the middle of the living room floor watching television when this white cat just walked through the back door. The cat and I eyeballed one another and it moved as if on a mission walking very slowly towards me.

Johnny continued with his phone call as if he didn't see anything.

Fear kicked in as I jumped up and then screamed, "There's a cat in the house."

Johnny dropped the phone, and the cat sprinted past me into the other side of the house. I know my brother was concerned because he hung up the phone and agreed to help me search for the unwelcomed guest.

Six of us could not find the cat and slowly everyone returned to his or her routine.

Later that night, I woke up from the weight of something heavy on my chest. I opened my eyes and saw the cat staring me right in the face. Again, I screamed. Then I grabbed a lamp, hit the cat with the lamp, and ran out of the room. On my way out, I saw the cat lying under the lamp on the bed.

Of course, my screaming woke up everyone in the house.

"What is it, Robbie?"

"I found the cat and I think I killed it," I yelled.

But when we entered my room, the cat was gone. The lamp was there, but not the cat.

"Maybe you just stunned it," Johnny said. "And it woke up and went out the window."

"Maybe it was just a dream," Loretta offered.

I knew better and was restless for months. I tried to hang out in my brother's room as much as possible. In my heart, I knew that it was just a matter of time before something bad happened to someone in our family.

Later, my stepfather was hospitalized for hepatitis. In the process of his crossing over transition, he decided to visit the person he liked the least and that so happen to be me. He came in the form of a black cat. The cat had green eyes, and in my stepfather's voice told me to, "Wake up!" I did not have any love for my stepfather when I was awake, and sure didn't have any for him while asleep.

The more I told him no, it seems the more agitated the cat became. I woke up crying and woke Loretta up. I was really afraid. Crying, I said, "Loretta, Nelson is dead."

"Leave me alone," Loretta said and hit me for waking her up.

I laid down under her trying to crawl in her back for protection. But she pushed me out the bed.

I stayed up the rest of the night on watch, scared, but on watch until finally morning came.

"Who are you calling Yaya," I asked as she picked up the phone.

"I'm calling the hospital to check on Nelson," she said.

"Oh," I said casually, "Nelson is dead."

I'll never forget her face. There was sheer terror in her eyes. Her lips trembled and she held her heart as she slowly sank to the floor. Her mouth was open, but there was no sound. Then the phone fell to the floor and made a loud thud. The steel chair she was sitting in earlier fell over from the weight she put on it and the crashing sound was deafening.

"Yaya," I screamed. I thought she was having a heart attack.

I was close. Yaya suffered a pain attack. Her spirit was filled with pain and unbelievable sadness.

Yaya was so beautiful, and it troubled my little soul to witness her suffering.

Everyone surrounded Yaya with an urgency to protect her.

Loretta beat the shit out of me.

Yaya regrouped. She slowly picked up the phone and cradled it near her heart as she called the hospital.

She was informed that indeed Nelson had crossed over two days ago and that they hadn't known how to get in touch with her.

Yaya was so sad for a long time.

My brothers and sisters started calling me the African Witch and kept me locked away in the bedroom. They had a field day kicking my ass whenever they felt like it.

After a few days, Yaya realized that I was absent.

It was an interesting time because I usually fight back and wasn't afraid of my older siblings, but I somehow felt that this was poetic justice.

Eyewitness

It was here, The Border, where my innocence was penetrated, my childhood times were violated, and a part of me went missing.

I was a dirty, stinky, little kid racing my friends, making mud pies, jumping from roof to roof, and scaling houses in gangways.

My favorite game was Cricket. We lined empty soda and beer cans up on each end. We even used cans to play street bowling. Our world was filled with magic.

I lived out loud, laughed, surrounded by all I knew as a child, clearly unsuspecting of the suspect.

When Ronnie and Pewee approached me and told me that my sister Gertrude directed them to quickly escort me home, the first thing that crossed my mind was that something had happened to Yaya.

Bewildered, totally blind to the danger that just had entered my world, I voluntarily mixed in their company. In all my eleven years of innocence, I was trusting, thinking I was safe in my community with my protective big brothers.

We took short cuts through familiar neighborhoods.

Suddenly, I was in an empty building.

I was shocked as they held me down and poured liquor down my throat.

How could this be? They are my sister's best friend's brothers.

Strength was summoned from fear, as my eighty-pound frame fought fiercely, but to no avail. A part of me abandoned my body and stepped outside to watch in terror the unimaginable violation.

I blacked out from this abysmal pain, screaming, and came to, only to black out again from the terror.

The police found me because a neighbor called them twice, persistent, saying she heard a girl screaming.

However, they took me to jail instead of the hospital.

Lost, hurt, confused, unloved, I sat in jail for a week, dirty, bloody, and stinky, before my sister Loretta fetched me. My soul was filled with shame.

I didn't understand why I was locked up.

What had I done to deserve this?

I was eleven.

No one was there to tell me that it was going to be ok.

The indescribable pain made me walk funny and bleed.

Why was I bleeding? Did they cut me? Is this what happens when you turn eleven?

Eleven. I hate that number, and everything associated with it. ELEVEN!

Home didn't look or feel the same.

After a long bath, Loretta took me to the emergency room. I was leaning in her arms.

This white doctor in a white coat asked, "What's wrong with her?"

"She was raped," Loretta replied.

"There is nothing wrong with her, don't waste my time. Get out of here."

My shame went deeper. Can you double break a heart?

I just knew that my heart couldn't take any more abuse.

What was wrong with me? What did I do? Why did everybody hate me?

Withdrawn, my room became my sanctuary.

Loretta finally took me to see Dr. Mitchell and Dr. Grant, our family doctors. They confirmed my violation. I was scarred with some internal damage. I don't know to what extent. They had no idea how deep the internal damage had traveled.

It wasn't just physical. I was damaged mentally and spiritually.

Consequently, I grew up fast, living in the midst of betrayal by family and friends. It wasn't like the police gave a shit about the molestation of a young, black female.

Yaya taught me that the greatest part of my self-validation is the core of transformation, quick to fight, with a moral compass, not to be trifled with.

I have made my way in this world from humble beginnings.

I never got to meet Yaya's full potential, being the product of my parent's broken promise, unfulfilled dreams, and their lover's dance. But the seeds she planted encouraged me to meet mine.

My life lessons began at age eleven. My first down fall and break through to the cutting edge.

Pieces of Life

At the age of eleven, my life had taken another serious turn of events.

Yaya suffered a stroke during heart surgery at the age of 42. She was at St. Catherine Hospital in East Chicago, Indiana. The doctor said she'd never come home again. This was a tremendous blow as my big *ole* world began to shrink.

My most endearing mission became finding my way to the hospital from Gary, Indiana to East Chicago. Yaya was in Intensive Care at St. Catherine. The waiting area for family members of Intensive Care patients was different than a normal hospital waiting room. I was prepared for a few days with a change of clothes.

The nurses allowed me to shower in an empty room. I had access to snacks and sometimes they would bring me food from the cafeteria or home.

As I stood in life's combat zone, pre-adolescent, filled with apprehension, futureless, and weeping, my thoughts were consumed with the question, "What the hell am I going to do?"

The fight to survive had begun.

I'd been there nearly a week before my sister Loretta came to visit Yaya and found me. Loretta was about eighteen. She was happy and not completely surprised to see me. She warned me that Gertrude would go for the kill when she saw me.

When we returned home, Gertrude busted me upside my head and called me all kinds of names.

After two days of abuse, I made my way back to the hospital. I needed Yaya so bad.

Three days later, the police arrived at the hospital and escorted me home 'pon Gertrude's directive.

They attempted to scare me about the streets, telling me about the awful things that could happen to me.

They were clueless.

We had our own private hell in my sister's household. If people only they knew the crazy shit she did to us. She'd strip us down and whip us with the *stenchen* (extension) cords.

Lizbeth

Lizbeth was my favorite sibling; I think she was the entire cousin's favorite and she was beautiful both inside and out. She had this infectious laugh, she made life look fun and I couldn't wait to be a teenager like her. She was the true dancer of my female siblings. She too loved music and taught me to close my eye listen to the beats and let my body dance.

It's interesting because Gertrude had the elementary education and was a great artist and a commanding voice. She could sing and write poetry. Lizbeth danced as if the drums commanded her body, she was partial to South America and African music as am I. She was the nurturer and in Yaya's absence she watched closely over me. I don't know if she was academically inclined like Loretta was, because she took sick at age fourteen and never recovered, we lost her at age nineteen.

Johnny

Johnny known as James Brown number two loved to sing and dance. He walked like James Brown except he was muscular, built broad chested, short, bow legged, pigeon toed and fun. Peaches was his favorite because she and Vincent could blow (sing), not me, although I knew all the songs.

We had contests who could name the most songs and he would give us a dollar, 10 cents for each song. I was fierce and very competitive, instead of my siblings naming the song they would sing with him. He always threw in some Hank Williams and Elvis Presley. He was a smooth dresser and designed clothes, but after he returned from Vietnam his light was gone.

JR

JR was the youngest; he was short also and built. He had a great sense of humor and loved to laugh. He always reminded me of Eddie Murphy. I used to tell him if he wasn't so short he could play Eddie. He also loved to dance and he loved Calypso, Salsa, and the Cha-Cha-Cha. We all danced the Cha-Cha-Cha. He escaped Gertrude by entering the Marines. He had a rough childhood and I am not sure the Military was the best place to recover from his childhood.

Like me, my brother loved to drive fast, we both used to always get speeding tickets. I relocated from Albuquerque, New Mexico to Topeka, Kansas and he relocated from Albuquerque to Taos, New Mexico. While returning home late one night he wrapped his car around a tree a week before he was to turn 36. I often wonder if it was on purpose. When he relocated from North, Carolina to Albuquerque in the mid 90's and we often talked about losing Yaya I was eleven he had to be seven or eight. When he shared his narratives of the abuse he suffered at the hands of Gertrude, I felt so ashamed for leaving him behind. I can only ask for his forgiveness.

Peaches

Gertrude would make my youngest sister, Peaches, run in place and leisurely punch her chest with her fist.

Peaches was a thick, heavy-set child. My baby sister would stand and run in place and become a punching bag, while tears streamed down her cheeks. Gertrude said this would make Peaches lose weight.

Peaches knew from experience that there was no sense of seeking mercy from Gertrude. She just endured the abuse until Gertrude became exhausted from beating her.

Vincent

My poor brother, Vincent, was knocked in the head with a hammer or tied up in a chair and whipped until his skin broke. He repeatedly called himself retarded because Gertrude told him so. But he was good with numbers like Yaya and he processed like me. He was a thinker and because we tended to take our time replying to questions, people thought we were slow.

Gertrude

Gertrude was Yaya's oldest child. She was high maintenance and very creative. She and our brother Johnny designed clothes for fun. Gertrude had an eye for fashion and loved to wear fancy clothes. She dressed to the T and so did Johnny.

While Gertrude was small, her personality was big. She was different, very beautiful, and the leader of her pack.

She was very convincing and had a small following. Because of her strong personality, she was able to influence people to do whatever she commanded.

Gertrude knew she was the product of rape and she was so angry at Yaya.

Yet, the community accepted her, and she was loved just the same.

We didn't throw away children.

Although she didn't want it, she had good, fine, white folk's hair, and she was pretty. Her European features were prominent.

Loretta

Loretta was eager to please Gertrude and did almost whatever she was ordered. She had her first child at an early age because Gertrude informed her it was alright to have sex. Loretta was the most passive with a very soft voice, and she lived in books. She was smart and loved learning, yet naïve because she adored Gertrude, and even I knew that was dangerous. Although third of the first four, I get the feeling she never really got to grow up. She had this pretty, smooth, coco skin, short hair, and was pigeon toed and very shapely.

In the beginning, when we lived on 13th and Adams, Gertrude was in charge of us while Yaya worked as a nanny in Chicago. Yaya would catch the South Shore train from Gary, Indiana to Chicago, Illinois on Sunday and return to us early on Friday.

Gertrude was good at manipulating and bullying us. I stayed at the hospital for five days, going over my short life. Sometimes, the nurses would buy me something to eat.

Sometimes, Gertrude would beat my three younger siblings to control me. The best thing for them was for me to disappear, I decided.

Gertrude reported me as a runaway. Thus, my lawless career began.

A Mixed Family

On one end of the block was the Jane Adams Settlement House, an after-school facility where we hung out throughout the week. However, all my activities were outdoors. I learned to play cricket. We found a flat stick, lined cans up, and used a baseball, tennis ball, and any small round ball we could find. We played marbles on the sidewalk. I collected marbles then and still today. We also pitched pennies to see how far we could get them over the sidewalk line. We bowled with plastic bottles and played dodgeball.

We also read comic books. I have a trunk filled with old comic books left over from my childhood.

Our family was mixed with everyone: Black, White, Creole, Puerto Rican, and Brazilian. We listened to all types of strange music, as the neighbors would say.

We lived in between the Roberts and the Walkers. I remember Sadie, Demetrius, and Derrick Walker very well. The Walkers were busy bodies and forever messing with people. This was ironic because my baby sister, Peaches, had a tendency to pick at people as well.

It helped being a tomboy and having quite a few male cousins in and out the house. As a child, I was very small in stature and had the ability to scale walls, the side of buildings, and people.

Peaches was plump when we were children and is *really* huge now. She is still funny, loving, shining, and struggling for a better life. It was a Saturday afternoon when Peaches came busting in the house, informing me that the Walkers were picking on her. It never occurred to me to ask Peaches what she did to them. No, this was my baby sister who was twice bigger than me.

I rushed out of the house with a belt in my hand and went over to the Walkers and, without pause, started slinging the belt.

Sadie, Demetrius, and Derrick were all wailing when their mother came outside. She was laughing while pulling me off her children. All three were older than me.

When Mrs. Walker took the belt from me, all three of the kids dived at me, but I somehow managed to keep them at bay. She took me home and reported my activities to my sister Gertrude.

Gertrude called Peaches into the living room and asked her what happened.

"Peaches," Gertrude said clearly frustrated with her younger sibling. "What happened?"

In Gertrude's mind Peaches' excuse wasn't good enough.

"Go into the bedroom," Gertrude instructed. "You're getting a whipping."

I don't know why Gertrude told her that. Peaches didn't take too kindly to whippings. She started whining right there on the spot before she'd been hit.

"Are you going to get some rest first?" I asked Gertrude.

"Why are you asking me that?" Gertrude asked, with a look of confusion. She had no idea what I meant.

When Gertrude entered the bedroom Peaches, dived under the bed. It was queen sized with two mattresses and a steel box spring. Gertrude tried to pull Peaches from under the bed, but Peaches was moving around, wailing, taking the bed with her. She was literally holding on to the bed and pulling it across the room!

It was unbelievable the strength of this girl. She was so afraid of whippings but was *always* into something, although sometimes it was my fault.

The unspoken rule was whenever Yaya or Gertrude lined us up for whippings, we would let Peaches go first, because they would be dog-tired after trying to whip her. Sometimes I'd feel sorry for them and say, "Give me my whipping first so I can get this over with."

Well, Peaches finally scrambled from under the bed screaming to the top of her lungs and hadn't been touched yet. She ran into the closet and scaled the wall all the way to the ceiling. I had taught my siblings to scale the walls with their hands and feet. I couldn't imagine what she was holding onto. Gertrude was highly pissed and determined to get at least one lick in.

Peaches was growling at Gertrude when Yaya came home, and Vincent ran to meet Yaya to tell her what was going on. Yaya walked into the bedroom, moved Gertrude out the way, reached up in that closet, and snatched Peaches right down.

By then, Peaches had peed on herself and Gertrude was too exhausted to continue the struggle.

The Walkers returned the payment to me in full the following week.

They bombed me with dirt balls as I was walking through our gangway. They lit me up. Dirt was all in my hair, face, and some of the balls had rocks in them. It was only fair. I thought it was original and I held no grudges. Soon after, we all became good friends.

Their Yaya really liked me and enjoyed having me around.

Everybody knew that Peaches was the shit starter and I would come in behind her to clean it up. As children, we still had to fight our way through a male domineering world. If my baby sister said it, then I enforced it.

Trying Times

6848 East 3rd Avenue, Miller, Indiana.

Gertrude and her husband had our home built in Miller, an up and coming suburb of Gary, Indiana. We actually lived around the corner and up the street from Wirt High School. Third avenue blocks were longer than dirt roads in Mississippi. At one end was the development of new homes and at the other was Miller Projects.

Gertrude had tried every religion. She was once sanctified. She had used Reverend Ike's red cloth to lay on us when she prayed. She was a Jehovah Witness until she wore them out, and then she was Baptist once again. No matter the religion, you could still suffer a good cuss up and beat down.

Gertrude was always in a rage and cussing us up for some reason or none. She had a way with words that just stripped you of every ounce of confidence. When she finished, you felt her dirty fingerprints all over you.

A nice rainstorm was commenced as thunder sounded like the heart of Cuban drums and magical colors lit the sky. Beauty derived from lightening. My brother-in law, Judge, had actually brought me home after my two weeks absence from this toxic environment. It never mattered how long I was gone from home; I always managed to go to school.

I was thirteen, almost fourteen, in my freshman year and, on this particular night, it was my turn to feel Gertrude's wrath up close and personal.

Gertrude would make us fast for days with no food or drinks. We could only wet our lips with water.

Being the oldest, I felt it was my duty to care for my siblings when Gertrude wasn't. I worried after the kids all the time. In my heart, I knew this type of fasting couldn't be considered caring.

I gathered my siblings, nieces, and nephew and walked over to Ralph's Grocery Store in Miller. As we walked through the store, I made sandwiches and fed them all. We feasted on sandwiches, chips, and milk. After I was satisfied that their stomachs were filled, I'd take them home.

I'm certain the store clerks knew I was feeding them, but they never bothered us.

With a heavy heart, I asked God to forgive me for stealing. I learned how to cry inside. I learned how to walk and hold my head at a certain angle so that tears would run inside instead of outside.

Sometimes, I'd sleep at Phyllis, or on someone's patio, or in a car. My friends would sometimes sneak me in their house to shower and change clothes. Some pretended I came over early to walk to school with them. Their parents knew what was going on, and I'm convinced they said nothing and allowed me to hold onto what little dignity I had.

Anyway, on this particular night, Judge left around 9:30 PM to go to work at Inland Steel Mill. While testing my bath water, Gertrude entered, hauled off, and slapped the shit out of me.

I fell in the water, but this time, I came up swinging.

It was custom for us to just stand still and let her beat us. My reaction was different this time. My whole being just couldn't take anymore. So much anger and pain had been simmering.

We scraped until she backed up threatening to call the police.

I returned to my bath and put on some fresh clothes. 'Pon entering the upstairs den, she began to cuss me up again and eventually put me out. I stood outside the door in the rain for a while, thinking maybe one of my siblings would bring me a coat and my shoes like usual. Realizing it wasn't going to happen, I walked coatless and shoeless to the projects and went to one of my schoolmate's house. Phyllis and her family welcomed me. They always took care of me in my time of need, which was plentiful. They never asked any questions and almost all my childhood troubles were unspoken.

There were four of us girlfriends and none of their family members asked me why I was at their house so much.

They always welcomed me and treated me with love and kindness.

At nearly fourteen, it was time for me to take control of my life. Taking a stand with Gertrude signaled the end of the old guard and a new self-beginning.

I called *Baba* (Daddy) and when I heard his voice, I broke down and cried.

At this emotional outburst, everyone in the house was shocked and knew that this was serious. Through all the beatings, bruises on my face, scars on my legs from extension cords, and the many times Gertrude had put me out, I had never cried. The pain was written all over my face, but I never, ever cried.

Phyllis's mother held me from behind while I wept. She held the phone as Baba listened to my cries. They were coming from a place of deep violation. It felt like my body was convulsing.

After regrouping, I gave Baba directions for where to pick me up.

Phyllis's sister, Linda, gave me a coat and some shoes.

All eyes were sad when the family hugged and kissed me goodbye.

As I walked down that dark road in the rain and stood in the shelter of the neighborhood hangout spot, my future smelled so good.

It was nearly midnight when Baba, a friend of his named James, and my cousin Velma Mae arrived. We drove back to Michigan City, Indiana in silence. Velma Mae kept looking at me, smiling and Baba was turned sideways in the front seat looking back, silently taking in my features.

I was fascinated with Velma Mae's silhouette. It was long. She had the longest neck I'd ever seen. She was slim, dark, and looked like she stepped out of National Geographic.

She was so beautiful. I saw her beauty before I saw mine. Realizing I looked like her felt like home. Finally, I saw evidence of the origin of my strong, African features. Where once everyone had called me a "dark, ugly African," her entire spirit whispered, "Queen." We barely said a word between us, but as we walked into GrandYaya Littlebit's house, she informed me that her home was open if there was ever a need.

I had so many cousins, a foundation, and they loved me.

We all looked alike. We were really skinny, even the men were lean. They had this lilt in their voice; you could hear music, a rhythm, when they talked. Some of them talked so fast, people would constantly ask them to repeat themselves.

My summer was great until my brother-in-law, Judge, came to get me. His mother crossed over and Gertrude wanted me to represent the family and stand in her place at Ms. Pearl's homegoing. As soon as we buried Ms. Pearl, all the family members began to network and I met my brother-in-law's family members from

Rochester, NY, Atlanta, GA, and Memphis, TN. Some were school educators, Pastors, and lawmen. I had never seen Judge so happy. Gertrude always made him feel like crap and even though his sense of humor helped him get through tough times, he laughed a lot to mask his pain, something I was already familiar with.

Judge returned to work the next day and Gertrude lit into me.

As a matter of fact, she had me placed on probation the following week, alleging that I was incorrigible.

"You're going to be a whore," she predicted. "You'll have a house filled with kids, live off welfare, and become an alcoholic and drug addict. Why can't you be a nice girl like Jamie?"

We were nearly fourteen and Jamie already had a child.

My mind was spinning and I wanted my Yaya so bad the soul injury was excruciating.

Needless to say, my exit was plotted 'pon my calling Danny Rae in Michigan City.

Forty-five minutes later, he pulled up in the driveway. Gertrude was in the bedroom. My clothes were packed in the garage. I grabbed my clothes and went back to Michigan City.

I was done with Gertrude and the fucking race riots at Wirt High School.

Velma Mae took me in, but a couple of months later a neighbor came and told her that the police were looking for me.

They sent me from house to house hiding me and then they spirited me out of town and sent me down to the Delta with Cecil and other family members.

This move allowed me to spend more time with family on the McMillen Plantation and throughout the Delta.

Drunken Man

During a walkabout through Shaw in DC

He shuffled past me with a crooked leg and bowed head

Something from him was pulling on me

memories of time hands held by another

A dark silhouette saying dis, dis, dis my dawter

He never schooled the lil' girl on the fact of life

All she recalls of their silent being was the voice of others

Lawd, she da spittin' image of your wife

Strolling down two-five in the City of GI (Gary, Indiana)

She catches a glimpse of a soul that captures her time

Hunched shoulders smell of urine and crouched real low,

the man who wants to be invisible

Reminds her of another with the Frederick Douglas Afro

She carries the unspoken words that filled the silence

With the man who held her hand

One day in Michigan City, Indiana

down the back alley she goes

She heard angry shouts,

cruel words fall on the drunken man

Like a mad child, she screams in terror

Ripping through the circle in a rage

Eyes on fire, she dares anyone to come forth

She was itching to engage

Life Stricken, motivated by unknown pain

To others her bold action spoke of one insane

All the while, the girl lioness

Protects the drunken man

One questions, who is he to you?

He is just a drunken fool

With raining eyes of pride and heart of sadness

Gently gripping the hand of the drunken man

Unashamed and undeterred she screams in their face

Dis, dis, dis, my DAD!

Mississippi Roots

Going back yonder wasn't all that hard. I carry good and bad memories.

I am stock of mine people and while most of them were raised in the Southern way, I just wasn't so eager to embrace the social ways of the South. The most frequent words thrown at me were, "Come here you lil' ole nappy headed Geeche."

While I didn't rightfully know what they were calling me, I knew it was nothing nice for the Buckras to be calling me that.

Times were hard then, even on children.

I used to wonder why we called our Grandyaya "Lilbit." Today, I know it was because that's all she had to give: a lil' bit of love, a lil' bit of food, and a lil' bit of herself.

There wasn't much room in those places called shacks (shotgun houses). There were cramped rooms with unrecognizable furniture, overflowing with people. When you found a bed, it was filled with bodies of all shapes, sizes, and smells - arms across faces and legs across hips.

I didn't get to know my Grandyaya much as a child and didn't get to understand her much as I got older. I do know she loved her some liquor and she loved men even more. She had a whole lot of babies for them. If memory serves me right, she had "two sets" and my Baba was from the first.

My father's name was Joelee White . His Baba's name was Napoleon White. Grandfather Napoleon was allegedly killed in a crap game in Greenwood, Mississippi.

Legend had it that my Baba was a changed man after the Korean War. His bloodline origins were via South Carolina. He was a Pullman Porter in Michigan City, Indiana. He was withdrawn and he slept with the silent killer (alcohol) until it came a calling.

It didn't matter what type of liquor it was; he was just glad to get a drink. The only time he talked was when he was full of liquor. I can't really say if stuttering was normal for him, because I never heard him speak when sober.

At least he talked when he was drunk. His brother, my Uncle Charles, would get drunk and sing all night long. You could hear Uncle Charles down the block singing, stuttering, and stumbling. We would be sitting outside the

Haborside Housing on benches and someone would say, "There goes Charles White. Ole Lawd, he's drunk and he's singing - the stuttering fool."

All the neighbors would get up, go inside, and lock their doors.

I didn't. I eagerly waited on Uncle Charles to make it to our complex and watch him as he knocked on everybody's door and sang. This was my entertainment for the evening.

I so admired Baba, he was like tainted fruit hanging from a tree, bent with unrest, rooted, bending, but not breaking. Baba loved Yaya hard as a two-fisted lover, he loved her to the very end.

Baba was a cat of different stripes. He was a quiet man, but it seems 'pon coming home from the Korean War that he was just plain silent. He watched everything, didn't speak much. He and all his siblings lived in the bottle. A few times, he strained shoe polish through some bread and drank it. He didn't bother anyone. He always had a book with him; he read a lot. He would introduce me all day to his friends if he was liquored up. The only time I heard him speak was when he was drunk and introducing me to his friends, "Dis dis, dis, dis, dis my dawter. Dis, dis, dis my dawter."

Baba's face was painted with pain. He wore the big Frederick Douglas Afro. He was well-built, with a broad chest, big shoulders, and bow-legged like James Brown. As a matter of fact, my mother was as bow-legged as Baba.

Although there was only 30 miles between us, years passed before I saw Baba. He may as well have lived in another country. The only time I saw him was when someone crossed over.

The last home-going and the last time I saw him was at Yaya's funeral. He lost it. I was young, but it broke my heart to witness his pain.

I can never know Yaya and Baba's pain. I could never walk in their shoes or carry the humiliation they carried with such dignity. They stood tall as an oak.

Then one day, I witnessed the silent scream.

Yep, life took my GrandYaya *Lilbit*, doubled her over, and she took what life dealt out to her. Yeah, she took it and began to live in a bottle.

Even as a child, viewing this world through the looking glass of my circumstances, I bore eyewitness to Jim Crow cripple Baba. Baba had quite a few monkeys on his back and I don't think they fell off just because they left the plantation.

How many silent screams can a family endure?

After years of watching our Baba crumble, Yaya bailed.

I have the utmost love and respect for her. She stepped out on her own to take care of eight children alone.

Looking back on the early days and listening to folks speak on my Baba, I gathered that he was really a decent man. I know from personal experience that he loved my Yaya as he cried over her often when drunk.

As a child, my biggest dream was my Baba coming to get me. One night, my fantasy became a reality and Baba came to my rescue.

Sankofa

Schlater, Mississippi: McMillen Plantation

Some years back in the early seventies, surrounded by the ancestors, a girlchild was summoned to Schlater, Mississippi for a journey in which was the beginning of her learning to explore the beauty in her bones.

It was strange returning to the plantation. The days were hot. It seems that the ground would rise up to meet you. Flies and mosquitoes convalesced, entirely too hot to fly or be active, occasionally moving as if inebriated.

Some of the McMillen kids watched me all the time, acting as if they were afraid of me. Old man McMillen talked to me through other people, always sending me messages, wanting to know if I needed anything.

I had no problem staring him down when we encountered each other. The anger still brewed in me. I remembered the things they did.

He would just tilt his head and stare, never uttered a word or sound. Not even a sigh.

"Old Man McMillen is looking at a ghost," someone explained to me. "You walk like Yaya. You favor her and Lizbeth."

It was true. I did look like them. I just courted darker skin, except I didn't consider myself beautiful like people considered them.

Although my elder sister Gertrude was a McMillen, the old man was compelled to stare. He never asked after her, Yaya, or Lizbeth. He knew our families that lived on that plantation, the Whites, Morgens, Harris's, Kings, and Thomas's, along with the Winston's and other families.

I wonder if he remembered as much as I did. I remembered he made Grandyaya Lilbit beat my three male cousins, Don, Pune, and Cat. She had to strap beat the boys all the time and afterwards you would see her crying and drinking.

No wonder all of them began to live in the bottle. And all my male cousins dated white women and two of them married white women. Sometimes, I wonder if it was because of their experience on the Plantation?

I harbored resentment for how my cousins were treated. I had a habit of making mean ass white people move when I didn't like them. Or, moreover, when they didn't like us.

I *imagined* that the best way to make them move was to burn their house down when everyone left for the day. The parents went to work, and the children were no longer allowed to play with us because we had to learn our place. So, I *imagined* their place had to be somewhere else besides next door.

Judy, her daughter Lynette, and I stayed in a trailer on the plantation. There were no Light Poles, just dark ass roads. So, at night, we had to use flashlights to see.

One night while I slept in the living room of the trailer, the door opened. A shadow was standing over me and a voice said, "Robbie, come go with me."

Everything seemed foggy and it was as if I was in a trance or drugged. I didn't know that voice; it didn't register at all. The shadow didn't touch me or say, "Get up." It just stood there in this long coat, and it was too hot for a coat.

Earlier, while lying on this same couch, there had been crickets and bull frogs serenading me. But now it was quiet, too quiet for my liking. My heart began racing as I failed to understand what was going on. My limbs grew heavy and I found I couldn't move them as I attempted to wave the shadow away.

The shadow bent closer to me and said, "Robbie, come go with me."

No one here knew me as Robbie, so right away I knew this couldn't be someone 'close by.'

Even though the figure hovered over me and a voice whispered in my ear, there was neither wind nor odor coming from the shadow. A chill went through me and I was rendered helpless, still trying to resist.

I heard the voice, saw the coat and hat, but not a face, as the shadow slowly moved down the hall towards the room where Judy was.

The shadow spoke to Judy. She responded but she was talking so loud and so fast. The words tumbling out her mouth was incomprehensible.

The shadowy figure retraced its steps and walked out the door.

Right away, Judy came running down the hall just as I was sitting up.

"Who was that?" Judy's eyes were wide.

"I don't know," I said, just as afraid as she was.

We both ran out the door after the person. The dark road was empty. There were no cars or people. Judy and I tried to figure out who it was. We didn't understand why the person was in a long coat on this hot evening. We never mentioned this incident again, just kept it close to our chests.

I had many experiences like that in both the North and South. I knew we had a visitor, can't tell you what kind, but it was fishing, and we didn't bite.

It wasn't long before I found many other reasons to leave Schlater, Mississippi to live with family in Greenwood, Mississippi where my favorite cousins lived.

My Name Is Not Fair Game!

You can lock me in

You can't lock me down

My mind is strong, operable, and sound

I am not content

With your new technology of enslavement

You see I hear a word there

An echo here, a whisper about

Lynchings, rape, and soul larceny

With your evil dealings

I came into being dark as midnight

That doesn't make it justice

With you denying me of and taking away my rights

Fourteen
Embedded Southern Culture

I got in trouble with white people and was too ignorant to realize the severity of it, but my cousins, family, and friends knew immediately.

While in a Juke Joint with my cousins in Greenwood, Mississippi, a white man touched my chest and I swatted his hand away. He then grabbed my back side and I hit his hand. My skin touched his skin. He drew back with a pool stick and my cousins and friends surrounded me.

"Don't mind her, Mister," they screamed in terror. "She's from up North and don't know any better."

I smelled the same fear on them that I had smelled on my sister when we got caught on the wrong side of town returning from night school in Gary, Indiana.

They convinced the man to let me go and once we returned to the adults, my cousins told them want happened. They made phone calls and the cousins came from Schlater to Greenwood, Mississippi to get me.

"Get her the hell out of here," the adults said. "She can't stay here no more."

And just like that, the very next morning, my cousin Darrell and I were headed to Florida. We were recruited to go pick oranges in Umatilla, Florida at Golden Gems Camp. Neither of us knew what to expect.

To be sure I wasn't recognized as a girl, we shaved my hair and since my chest was flat, I was a pretty, quiet boy. People actually kept their distance because they thought I was gay, due to my walk.

I was no stranger to hard work. I'd picked cotton and pecans now and then in Mississippi to earn my own money. I used it to help out with bills and groceries wherever I stayed. Most of the time, it was just pocket money, only enough to feed myself.

Now here I was at the age of fourteen, a migrant worker in Umatilla, Florida, picking crates of oranges and grapefruits.

When my gender could no longer be hidden, cousin Darrell ordered everyone to keep their distance or they would answer to him. Since he didn't mind a good fight, we were fighting all the time.

A family member informed Gertrude of my whereabouts. She contacted the police and I was returned to Gary, Indiana.

There I was sitting in Juvenile Court.

While I was locked up, Yaya was visiting my mind. I was thinking about our heroes. You see, Yaya loved to watch cowboy movies, and since there were no images of black men on television, we'd watch Randolph Scott, James Stewart, John Wayne, Lee Marvin, and Audie Murphy.

I was drawn to Audie Murphy because, although he seemed to have a limp, he always ended on top. My favorite hero was Yul Brynner. He didn't take any shit, and I personally thought if he had to defend me, it would be someone's misfortune. I dreamt of him protecting us against the atrocious deed of others.

As it turns out, the real hero was in the courtroom with me. Uncle T, also known as Passing T due to his skilled gambling abilities, drove thirty miles from Michigan City, Indiana to Gary, Indiana to stand in on behalf of my mother and father.

After two weeks in Crown Point Detention Center, my co-conspirator, Gloria, and I broke out. Wearing detention issue jump suits and gym shoes, we somehow managed to get outdoors. We swiped 'street clothes' off the clothing lines and hitchhiked from Crown Point to Gary, Indiana.

A gentleman returning from fishing picked us up and we somehow managed to get pass the police roadblock. Once we returned to Gary, Indiana, I called for a ride to Michigan City.

You always return to what is familiar to you.

There was a fire brewing in me, and it just couldn't keep still.

All that I knew

Last night his strong hand pulled me to him

Announcing the wanting of my naked body

His incredible soft lips were everywhere

Chasing the daily pain away, his arms enfolded my body

Into his fortress of love as his hands

Molded, urgently massaged mine breast, mine back,

mine onion,

Mine thighs, as his fingers traveled

in search of my triangle of love

His enchanting hands serenaded mine body

His low moans against my neck, in mine belly button

The heavy breathing was galvanizing

I took him in with mine eyes that witnessed

The cascades of love consume him

He filled the room and all that I knew was him

Mine hip did a slow grind against his backside

His manhood throbbed, standing erect

He reached back and pulled

Me closer for more up-against-the-wall love

My performance called for me

to face mine opponent again

Lawd loving like dis is just a sin

We engaged and dined on one another

Hips locked; bodies rocked

Dancing a dance of sweet romance and then

His ripping embrace and muffled groans told me when

All that I knew was him

All that I saw was him

All that I heard was him

As mine man fell into a

Deep drug like sleep

Meeting Myself

Memories surface when he called back in the day. He was in Gary, Indiana and I was in Albuquerque, New Mexico.

"Just touching base," he said, "wanted to hear your voice."

His laugh was genuine, soft, and warm. It reminded me of old times, when we were one. I listened as he reminisced on our first encounter.

"I was mesmerized by your stroll," he said. "I'd never seen a woman walk with their whole body."

"I remember," I said slowly. "You were being rude."

James had been hanging out of his car, flirting with time.

"You were always feisty and had a bad attitude. You spoke so fast; I couldn't help wanting to know more."

I didn't respond. I was too busy living in the memory he painted.

"I needed a friend," he said sadly. "I miss the smells you added to my life – your cooking, your cleaning, your loving."

Still, I remained silent.

"You still dance," he asked. "I always loved watching you dance."

I laughed and he went on.

"Do you still twist your lips? I love your lopsided dimple smile." He exhaled. "I miss watching you stroll. I'd know your sashay anywhere."

And then, finally, he decided to give it to me straight.

"I'm sorry, Robbie."

"For what?" I wanted to know. Did he get it?

"For my wayward habits," he confessed. "I miss you so much it hurts."

I felt and heard the pain ebbing from his soul. His voice was piercing.

"I'm not doing drugs anymore," he said quietly.

"You're not doing drugs *as much* anymore," I corrected.

We sat holding the phone with a pregnant pause before he replied.

"Yes, not doing drugs as much anymore."

Holding the phone knuckle tight, I felt the fat man sitting on my chest, caving my heart.

Once you go forward, you can't go back.

I grew up and he remained the same. I moved on and he continued to live in a vacuum.

Hear me this, I love my people. African Americans are the most amazing, original group of people on this earth. Often, I'm told that I love my culture and my people too much.

I have to break, step back, and ask, "How is that possible?"

James's phone call took me back to the spring of 1975.

Recently emancipated from Indiana Girls School, Indianapolis Indiana, I was sitting on the stoop, French braiding my niece's hair. My nephew sat, waiting his turn, and my mind was a world away from where I was just a month earlier.

A young man pulled up in a Red Nine-Eight Oldsmobile.

"How much you charge to do mine?"

Since he was hairless, the assumption was that he asked on behalf of someone else. I'd braided hair since I was a child. We females took turns grooming each other and we never charged, so it was strange that he asked.

My face answered his question.

He then unfolded himself from the car and, *wow*, this tall slice of Carmel Cake stood before me and my eyes refused to leave his six-foot frame. My mind reached back, and I knew he was the brother hollering at me the other day.

Leaning against the car, arms folded, he said, "My name is James Davis. They call me Jimmy D or Slim."

I smiled.

"The polite thing to do is tell me yours," he said leaning forward with such confidence. "I just need your first name. Already know your last name will be Davis."

My nephew remained silent, but he was breathing like a bull. He eyed James suspiciously, while my tongue was tied. I heard my nieces simultaneously, in their innocent voices, excitedly introduce me. "This is Auntie Robbie," and then they were nothing but teeth and giggles.

James courted the girls, asked their names, and gently secured their background information, while my nephew's suspicions turned to a frown. He called on the courage to ask James personal questions. The girls shut their brother down and pulled him away as James asked to speak to me in private.

Excused by the family, we walked down 17th of Massachusetts Street slowly for a while before he spoke again.

My heart was racing.

"Are you involved with someone," he asked.

Catching my breath, I faintly replied, "Yes."

Not knowing what to expect, he said, "All right, I'm going to wait until y'all split up, because if I take you from him, someone will take you from me, and you are a keeper."

James began to come around, and for at least five months we were friends. He hung around in the background, quietly becoming my best friend.

It'd been nearly six months since I had first blessed my eyes 'pon James, and our journey began. We were inseparable and discussed everything. James told me while a child in Brownsville, Tennessee, he watched beautiful women leave for the big cities only to return later in ruin, drug and alcohol ridden, overwhelmed with children, and some stepped out of their mind.

"God, if you give me one of them, I promise, I will take care of them," he promised.

"When I saw you walking down 35th Avenue, I almost wrecked and had to turn around and offer you a ride. I apologize for being rude."

He said he knew it was fate, to see me again twice within a week.

James looked me in the eyes and said, "I'm going to take care of you as best I can, but promise me, if I start abusing you, you will leave. I don't want anybody to make a fool of you. Not even me."

There I was, seventeen-years-old, motherless, no education, no job prospects, and this twenty-one-year-old was openly declaring his love for me, and I grew in his love.

All my childhood elders were gone. There was no one to go to for womanly advice.

Loretta opened her home to me and afforded my emancipation from Indiana Girl's School to her, but she didn't really expect me to stay with her. She and her husband had a one-bedroom apartment, five children, and two of my younger siblings. They made room for me, even when there was none.

The new journey was exciting. I was around my siblings without worrying about being in trouble. I had no clue what opportunities were to come and yet I was still looking forward to the future.

James asked me to move in with him. Of course, Loretta was so glad to get me out of her house. Needless to say, I moved in. He had no idea what he was in for. He gently held me through the nightmares, and patiently talked me through some trying times.

One day, while conversing, he said with such surprise, "You know you're green, really green."

Years later I realized what he meant; I knew nothing about men and women, making love, or being in a *real* relationship.

Life was good. James and I lived on 21st Washington in a nice apartment with new furniture. Here I was at nineteen, having my first child and securing my GED.

This particular day, I was in the house cooking goat. James and our friend Dillion were en route after making a beer run. I heard a commotion outside and witnessed a crowd of people in the street looking at the building and pointing at the window.

Wailing emergency sirens drew near as fire singed the walls in the hallway and traveled from the back staircase. Without hesitation, I ran down the flight of stairs. James and Dillion met me at the entrance.

They both grabbed unto me, their eyes loaded with fear. I stood between my protectors as we walked out to the street. The previous day, James had taken me shopping for maternity clothes. Although I was five months, my stomach was barely a bump.

As the fire reached the living room, the three of us stood watching.

"There goes the living room," I said.

"There goes the bedroom," James said.

Dillion joked, "Well, Robbie, I guess we will never get to eat your goat."

We laughed at this unknown curve. We had no idea a reporter was standing next to us. All we knew was this tall white guy was being nice, asking us questions, including our names. Although our story was in the newspaper, we didn't get any help from the American Red Cross, or any other social service group.

We stayed with friends and I went to school the next day as if nothing happened.

Two days later, my stomach blew up! Oh boy! I was wobbling with swollen feet that refused to fit in my shoes. My feet were spilling over like sausages.

I just borrowed clothes from friends that were too big for me, including shoes, and I went to school.

A few months later, I received my GED and on July 9th, 1977, my father crossed over and my first child was born.

Shot Caller

We lived on 19th of Connecticut in 1977.

My son was born in July and barely a month old, but was trying to sit up, moving around, pulling himself across the bed. He was left in his daddy and my sister's charge when I visited Mr. Bobs, our neighborhood corner store on 18th avenue.

While in the store purchasing household items, a young man began flirting with me. He boldly commented on my breast and asked me to sit on his face.

When he talked *under my clothes*, I mouthed off to him. I was embarrassed (and I don't embarrass easily) but even then I knew how important it was for women to take up for themselves all the time.

"A real man don't need to announce or inflate himself," I said. "If you don't have no bedside manners, you have no command in bed."

He was quiet as everybody laughed. His eyes grew cold and his glare sent a shiver over me.

No big deal. I got my things and went home. When I got home, my son was in the bedroom, sleeping. James, Peaches, my brother Vincent, and a few neighbors were playing spades as they normally did.

There was a disturbance outside our house.

James's mother ran *policy* (we call them numbers). She was a numbers runner in the building next door and his sister Jewell was there. Eugene Barker was outside my house calling for me. We all went outside. Eugene had brought his wife over to fight me.

"I don't want to fight her," Eugene's wife cried. "I don't know her."

"You can fight her or me," He told her.

"Man, this is not going down," James said.

In all my innocence, the wife rushed me, and I let her hit me once.

After that, every time my fist touched her face it involuntarily split open. She was bleeding and crying, but kept coming at me, because Eugene's dumb ass was threatening her.

I felt so bad. My stomach was sick, and I heard Yaya in my head saying, "Women don't fight women, they are supposed to take care of each other because no one else will."

Eugene went to his trunk, pulled out a machine gun, and pointed at my brother first. Vincent and Kerrie jumped the fence. Everyone ran but me. Not that I was brave but was in shock.

Eugene's partner in crime, Clay O'dell, pulled out a shotgun and hit me in the mouth with the butt.

"Run, you damn fool," Jewell screamed.

I ran in the house and they shot up the house. James was returning their fire with fire. As Clay unloaded the shotgun, I was hit with the buck shots. Peaches was hit three times from the Machine gun. She was pregnant.

Of course, the police arrived to find a mess. My sister was shot, and not only did she lose the baby, but she also lost a piece of her lung and a kidney. A bullet sits near her heart to this day.

Peaches was in the hospital for months.

I have some gangster-ass cousins. They came in from all over Michigan, Illinois, Wisconsin, Virginia, Louisiana, Mississippi, South Carolina, and New York, and they came to kill. Even the PG's from 22nd Avenue and Two-Five came to offer support. These gang members were willing to hook up with some of my family, their rival gang members, the Black Peace Stones, to support us.

There I was, 19, a new mother, and given the authority to call the shots.

This was a definitive moment in my life. Fighting was not a new phenomenon to us. We had to scrap all the time. I had a pretty bad reputation as a fighter, but I knew in my heart there was so much more to me than that. It was not the life I wanted for my children. I didn't want to be that type of shot caller.

Eugene and Clay were hemmed up at Clay's mother's house and there was no way I was going to let them shoot up that house with an innocent woman and children there. That blood would not be on my hands.

Family members stayed around like an army, escorting me everywhere. Some stayed at the hospital with my sister, Peaches. They sent word to Eugene, "Let's do it again, we are inviting you to come on by."

We had protection for three months, but I would not let them retaliate. This is not how I wanted to be remembered, ordering an execution. Needless to say, the police finally caught up with Eugene, who had killed a lot of people. He was a serial killer. Even knowing this, I could have ordered his execution and saved a few people. But that would have been on my conscience and I could not be the judge and executioner.

I realized that if I could bring rival gang members together, then I had the capacity to make something positive of it at the next opportunity.

This incident brought forth undisclosed prospects again, as I witnessed machine guns, Mack 9's, Thirty Eights and Forty Fives exchange hands in my house. I knew it was time to leave Gary, Indiana. After family and friends returned to their homeland, we moved to Decatur, Illinois where my second son was born on July 27th, 1979.

LET ME INTO YOU

Baaaaaby, open your chamber of emotions

As I enter your mind's palace

To bring forth a realm of passion

And dine on love conditionally

Let me, let me into you

Receive me with a peaceful sigh

Moving from the tightness and seriousness of self

While we dance the sensations

Of sensuous wealth

Fingers walk, bodies talk

Lips finesse a pearl of caress

That induces ripples of organisms

Illuminating our oneness

As you see me melt into you

I knew in my heart he couldn't make me feel that,

didn't have it in him to give me that

and I wrapped it up and let it go.

The Gypsy In Me
Michigan City, Indiana

James was working for the Railroad and I enrolled in Decatur Community College to take Criminal Justice courses. It was hell, being the only black student and female. I knew white people hated us; my classmates were sickly brutal. However, my instructor was very cool and understanding.

I was homesick and really needed to be with family. Appraising James of my need to be near family, we decided to move to Michigan City, Indiana. I informed my instructor of my decision. He asked me not to go and told me, "You got what it takes to be in the field of Criminal Justice."

I took that statement with me.

We moved to Michigan City, Indiana and I was surrounded by family.

My Aunt Gloria Mae was not taken to me in the beginning; she said I was too much like my mother. This is when I learned that not all our family loved Yaya.

"You're too much like Bobbie Ree," she said and frowned. "You walk like her, look like her, and fight like her too."

As much as Aunt Gloria Mae disliked me, my Aunt Willa Mae sometimes (called crazy Willa with her bad stutter and Gullahan) loved me. She allowed me to stay with her.

To my surprise, my cousin Gigi and I resembled each other so much that I was not admitted into department stores and some restaurants!

It was embarrassing when store clerks, the police, and security guards would approach me to escort me out the store, and I would have to show them my ID.

It turned out that Gigi was boosting three-piece suits, computers, housewares, and clothing. All you had to do was put in an order and she would confiscate it, practicing eminent domain.

It was the luck of a Geeche that I was able to enter the CETA program, a work study program similar to workforce development.

During the role play for an interview, the interviewer, Sydney Vaughn, asked me, "How do you feel about working with white people?"

"I feel good," I replied. "They're no better than me."

He laughed and said, "We are going to hire you."

Honestly, I had no idea what happened or who exactly *"we"* was. I mean, he was doing a favor for his wife, one of the CETA instructors, in role playing interviews.

True to his word, I received a phone call from Mr. Vaughn and then Mr. Jay Ivory. The goal was to hire me in maintenance under YACC (Young Adult Conservation Corp). 'Pon my arrival to the maintenance yard, they sent me to the Visitor Center. I was to work in the Environmental Education Division.

Once upon a time, alcohol ruled our family. Today, drugs are not only consuming our family, but literary expunging our precious bloodline. The one thing I refuse to compete with is the command of drugs.

James started chasing *Girl* (cocaine) when he went to Vietnam at age 18.

My father served in the Korean War and as the story goes, his face was coated differently 'pon his return, filled with so much sorrow and pain. My older brother served in Vietnam and he is certifiably crazy. My youngest brother served in the Marines and he was also gone too soon at age 35.

It's ironic how many of our men measure their manhood by going to war. Generations of our men fought for the respect and love of a country that will never applaud them for their heroic efforts and their lives are ruined by Narcotic Sue.

I was the other woman in a soulful, enriching, and often uncomplimentary relationship. His mistress's name was Narcotic Sue (drugs). They intertwined on a soaring soul melee, off and on a romantic, but disparaging, voyage. We were ten years into our relationship before I learned that he was sleeping with Narcotic Sue on a daily basis, he was in damn deep. He was a functioning Junkie, and there I was hearing his whispers, "Don't let me abuse you, don't let me use you." He had given me fair warning in the very beginning.

When I looked around everyone was getting high - the good church-going girls and the decent brothers. I had to wonder what the hell was going on. My greatest asset is that I've never been with the *in crowd*. Even as a child, I was the leader, hopping trains, jumping from windows to roofs, and scaling houses in gangways. I knew all my neighbors' business. Sometimes I would go sit on their roofs and watch the world goes by, knowing this city was too small for me.

The gypsy in me was strong.

My life was unbalanced but enriched with my sons. My day job at the Paul Douglas Center at Indiana Dunes National Lakeshore was rewarding, as my sons participated in a lot of the activities. I also worked as a counselor at the Alternative House Crises Center, and my sons went there as well. I attended Indiana University Northwest, and my sons either attended classes with me or hung out in the student lounge.

Was I too focused or just blind?

My summer vacations were spent at Oyo Tunja African Village in South Carolina or in New Orleans.

My sons preferred to stay in Michigan City with family. They considered these places foreign and forbidden, listening to society continue to strip us of our cultural traditions.

One thing I loved about James is that I feel he knew me. He never called me an African witch. He knew my religion was Yoruba and he never made fun of me. He accepted me and never tried to make me feel small.

James knew me by name (all of them) and how they were received: the naming ceremony with my elders - Oso' Tunde: The Seer Comes Again, and Oyo' Rinde: Joy Walks In. He even knew that my elders in the South called me *Sippianna* due to my rearing in Indiana, Mississippi, Louisiana and South Carolina.

As much as he knew me, there were some things he didn't know. James was losing it, going off, and when he tried to put his hands on me I would snap and crawl all over his ass. I'd move so fast, be there and back before he could blink. James wolfed a lot, screaming and threatening with his height. However, if he would get too close, I responded.

It took a while for me to understand that this was just his way of trying to intimidate me because most of the time, I was fearless and he meant me no harm.

My memory of my first fight at age eight, with the 16-year-old girl, is still with me. She slapped me (I don't recollect what for) and I scaled her ass. They had to pull me off her.

The second fight, I was nine. We lived at 222 West 11th Avenue, and Yalina and Willamina were picking at me. I took a switch to them and whipped them in circles until my sister, Loretta stopped me. They were fourteen and fifteen.

I have never feared a battle, physically, mentally, or spiritually.

James took me dancing every weekend. Sometimes, we went separately because he'd go to the gambling joints. We could dance with other people, but the rule was no slow dancing with others.

James was drowning in Narcotic Sue (drugs). I took him to a rehab three times in East Chicago, Indiana. However, our life changed one evening.

"You still here?" He asked as he slammed his fist on the dining table.

I changed the locks the very next day and put his belongings in the garage. This was another turning point in my life.

I realized that all our needs are the same. it's only our experiences that differs us.

James was still a good man, just hopelessly sprung.

Don't get me wrong, James and I shared many issues. We had our faults, faced numerous challenges and overcame plentiful obstacles. He was a good man with many burdens. I was no picnic, but was perhaps more grounded or focused than he, in that at least I knew what I didn't want.

I was working three jobs, not out of necessity, but because it kept me occupied and doing something. I enjoyed in working with youth. As a counselor, I was planning to get my counseling license through hours instead of school, but it never worked out as planned.

James brought me child support every month. His disability was his only source of income and yet he never made any excuses for paying it. I didn't want to take it. It made me feel greedy and selfish taking his money. The boys were alright; they were not hurting for anything. But he insisted. So, I put the money in the dresser drawer.

One evening James and his girlfriend, Mary, knocked on my side door.

"Can me and Mary sleep in your car in the garage?" he asked, looking like a ghost of someone I once loved.

It hurts to see someone you love looking and living like this. "No," I said firmly. "But wait here a minute."

I collected the money he had given me for child support from the dresser drawer and took them to a hotel. I then helped them get an apartment using more of the money he'd given me to pay the deposit and three months' rent. I figured they should have a game plan by then.

I was his first love and he mine. I will always love him, but I was no longer in his love.

James is due accolades; he was my love for over thirteen years and supported everything my heart desired. Although the last three years were challenging, I prefer to focus on the good.

Every year I spent a week in either New Orleans, Mississippi, or South Carolina and he would keep the boys. The creator blessed me early on in life to taste and experience love in action.

My experience will not allow me to settle for less.

I learned that some people will never know, have, or experience the magnetism of love. I am thankful for this experience. It set in motion my searching and discovering the essence of me and feeling the *Beauty In My Bones*.

James made me feel beautiful. I can still see the way his eyes lit up when he looked at me.

It took a long time for me to meet me and learn to appreciate the making of me.

James and I had that *up against the wall love* and would take it to the killing floor. We did some serious love making, bed shaking, it was something, yea. Sometimes, I can feel his presence and smell his cigarettes and it is powerful.

James survived the streets, but his body gave out on him, and in 2002, his girlfriend took him to the hospital. He had no insurance. He was in the emergency room all night and at *dayclean* (morning), he left the hospital, only for his stomach to erupt. He stood in front of the hospital, throwing up blood, and died.

I am grateful to have known him. He was, and still is, a very significant part of my life. He was my confidant, protector, teacher, and lover.

I hear every word that he wants to say. He will be mine tomorrow, but not today. Lean in my friend. Lean in!

If you are ever blessed to be in a soulmate's melody, I pray your memories are as rich as mine.

Uncle T

Uncle T was a man of small stature, but big presence. He was my *Little Giant*. He taught me so much in the name of family and honor. I loved that man, and although he is gone from this earth, he is still a very real part of me. He was a true warrior in my adolescent eyes, when he took on my sister Gertrude. He was also one to reckon with and wasn't afraid of her like everyone else.

The majority of my family is very temperamental – quick to anger and ready to battle verbally, mentally, and physically. This was true of Uncle T. My admiration was great as my eyes witnessed him stand toe to toe with her in the courtroom.

Uncle T's children were just as feisty as he was. I was very close with his two oldest daughters, Marleen and Red Bone. They embraced me with each visit and then we'd hang out in their bedroom, listening to the radio. Our favorite songs were *I Love You For So Many Reasons* by The Third Degrees, The Moments', *I Found Love On A Two Way Street*, and Wilson Pickett's *Midnight Hour*.

In February of 2000, Uncle T crossed over to the spirit world.

My breathing stopped.

Brandon jumped up, bent me over. "Breathe," he instructed. His voice was so far away.

Once my breathing became regular, I called home and spoke to Red Bone. She had already called and left a message for me to call. I knew we had lost someone and just didn't know exactly who. As she was talking to me, it was not registering right; my mind was spinning and refused to accept him being gone.

Eventually I began to focus in, and Red Bone shared the intended arrangements with me, "I'm on my way," I said.

Although Albuquerque was seven hours away and Phoenix was four, spiritually, I was compelled to fly out of Albuquerque.

I drove to Albuquerque two days later, only to find that there was a big snowstorm in Chicago and my flight was going to detour over to St. Louis. I kept calling home. I felt helpless and lonely because if there is anybody in the family I should've been there for, it was my Uncle T. I ended up spending the night with some friend in

Corrales, New Mexico. I laid on the futon in their living room thinking about my uncle and what a good man he was. His life was no bed of roses. He'd had a hard life, and yet, he continued to stand tall. When he was incarcerated, I would visit him every other month and write him monthly.

Uncle T was responsible for pointing our family North after a shootout with the McMillens.

One of the McMillens shot my Aunt Salina Mae and in retaliation, my uncles shot them up. Afterwards, Uncle T contacted every family member he could and encouraged them to head to Indiana, Michigan, or Chicago.

I recall all the times I went home (from Albuquerque, NM, New Orleans and Grand Canyon, AZ). I'd go over to Harborside Housing and visit my Uncle. His wife, Lorraine, would answer the door and holler, "T, it's your niece."

I'd speak to all his sons and then he and I would just sit on the stoop and talk. I'd bring him up to date with what was going on with me, and he'd let me know how he was doing with the cancer, not how the cancer was doing him. Sometimes, we'd just sit on the stoop and watch people in silence until it was time for me to go.

He was my true hero and the closest father figure I would ever know. He was brutally honest with me, treated me like I was his own, and jumped in my shit in a heartbeat if he felt I was screwing my life up. He asked after my sons all the time and would just talk with them while they were growing up.

Uncle T respectfully reminded me of my bloodline.

"You are Joelee and Snoop's daughter," he would say. Yaya's nickname was Snoop. "Invest in yourself. Believe in yourself. Don't forget where you came from."

A fit of sadness overwhelmed me, and my body just went into convulsions. I wept like a baby. I was on my knees, snot was slinging everywhere, and in between gathering my breath, I managed to lay my body down.

A rush of warmth entered the room and as I lay on my side in a fetal position, some unknown force hugged me until my spirit calmed down. I closed my eyes and felt my uncle's strong presence.

"Everything is alright," he told me.

I laid there for a while and he quietly went away.

"No matter how far you travel, stay connected to your kin, Robbie," Uncle T often reminded me. "It will keep your soul fortified."

Uncle T loved life. He lived hard and earned everything he had including respect. He was, and still is, my little giant.

The Visitor

The rain came down, cleansing the earth

Tuesday night while in quest for slumber

At the charming Sulphur Springs Inn

A visitor unseen to me was within

Taxing presence so unkind

Interrupting my dreams

Image tossing, body freeze, brain squeeze

None heard the ghastly screams

Escaping from the constricted voice box

Mind reeling, body dispirited

Doors locked, unanswered knocks

Stumbling grasping for security

Tried to shake, couldn't break

Mine visitor dragged me deeper and deeper

Mind wrapped around the creator

Ancestors summoned with all mine strength

Energy blast at last

The unwanted dispatched

Am I free?

As I rise weary and fatigued

From wrestling with a visitor unknown to me

Sulphur Springs Inn Oklahoma

In March of 2002, several colleagues and I attended a budget training workshop in Sulphur, Oklahoma. The atmosphere of this small, quaint town was heavy. I felt the undercurrents of the town's old history pulling in my gut and on the strings of my heart. The people were very warm and hospitable, and I was reminded of a town that the outside world forgot about.

We stayed at the Sulphur Springs Inn Bed & Breakfast. My room was on the second floor of the east wing. To my delight, the room was charming. It was decorated with a table, two chairs, and numerous books that captured my interest about women like Wilma Mankiller and Linda Hogan.

Sleep visited 'pon me fast that first night, because we'd been on the road since 4:00 AM and didn't arrive until well after midnight.

However, the second night as I lay down to rest, something was in the room, heavy on my chest. I was wrestling to get it off and screamed to the top of my lungs. The spiritual warfare was unwarranted and left me drained. However, I got my ass up and ran outside the room. While my colleagues were sleeping, I walked the halls and sat outside of my room on the floor.

The next day I told Mona, my colleague, about the visitor.

"You're welcome to come to my room," she offered.

But I declined.

On my third night there, the visitor returned in full force. I didn't want to be bothered. My heart was pumping fast and I couldn't focus to figure out what was really going on.

I knew something was going on with someone in my family, and it was beyond me why they were so anxious for me to know. After coming out of the trance, I ran down the hall to Mona's room. I stopped short of knocking on her door for fear of what she would think of me, or even say to me at this time of night. I bravely walked back down the hall, sat on the stairs for a while, and then finally reentered.

"Whatever is going on you can come to me better than this," I said braver than I felt. "You are scaring the shit out of me and I can't hear nor help you if I'm afraid."

The room warmed up and all was calm, and the visitor left.

'Pon returning home, I began calling all over to check on my family. I called Wisconsin, Florida, Virginia, Kansas, and Louisiana. Finally, I called my cousin Nini in Michigan City, Indiana and told her about my experience.

"It was your cousin Julie," Cousin Nini said quietly. "She died while shopping with her husband."

I couldn't believe my ears. Julie was young.

"They don't know what happened," Nini continued. "She just dropped."

There are so many of us and I have a genuine relationship with most of my family members. I hadn't seen Julie in years, but whenever I was in town, we somehow managed to run into one another, as if our paths were meant to cross.

Conclusion

Some years back, surrounded by the ancestors, a girlchild was summoned to forgive the sins for her family's enemy friend.

Even though we experienced a prohibition era in the 1920s, a society failed to market alcohol as a drug. Although it's the leading cause of death in this country, and has ruined many cultures, families, and businesses, I shouldn't complain since it's no longer the curse of my family. Crack and cocaine are my family's biggest enemies.

I didn't think much of growing up on a plantation. It seemed fitting to do whatever I wanted, since all my kinfolk were picking cotton. They told me I had a mind of my own that was no good and was just going to get me in real trouble or killed. It irritated the hell out of me to step off the sidewalk for those good folks! If they were such good folks, then what did that make us?

Folks say it ain't natural for a child to run wild like that. I say it ain't natural to be found frozen to death, naked in the summertime. They think I don't know about Uncle Pistol. I know and I'm still pretty damn mad. I say it ain't natural to take a human being and cut them up like sausage only to deliver him to his people.

Aunt Jane was always going around giving folks a piece of her mind. They say that one day her cup just runneth over, her mind left her, never to be found again.

They say Gertrude was crazy cause she didn't know who she was. I say she was just all twisted up inside 'cause she got one green eye and one brown eye. It doesn't make a difference. Everybody knows whose child she was.

Sometimes it doesn't make sense to know who you are, because you are not going to like yourself anyway. Some folks are born to be miserable for the rest of their lives.

I'll tell you what I do know today. I love my people. They are the most beautiful, courageous people you'd be blessed to meet. You see, my father and forefathers raised the children that were the result of the rape of their wives. They were the strong and silent type and just let the rage flow through them.

Have you ever seen a silent scream?

I am the oldest of the second set of children and can't rightfully say if I was a Baba's girl or not.

Quite honestly, a third adult was in the family and it was me.

The majestic Grand Canyon is my backyard. The patio is my sanctuary, as stillness surrounds me; many sounds greet me, as I am settling into stillness, marveling at my life fortunes, venturing through corridors of the canyon. The previous evening, I was witness to a white coyote. Years ago, Pauline taught me that it is bad luck for a Navajo Native American to face off with a Coyote. When we used to go walking in Petroglyph National Monument in Albuquerque, New Mexico, and venture 'pon a Coyote, I'd have to protect her and block her vison so that she would not fall 'pon bad fortunes.

Some people fall asleep to car's honking, car alarms, emergency sirens, or community activities. Others fall asleep to crickets or the flutter of birds. I fell asleep to the call of the Coyote, Elks bugling, and the stillness of night for seven years.

Alicia Keys's song "Wake Up" is in the background, a song with various messages which can set you back on reflection. Sometimes, we get lost in life's twists and turns and tend to lose bits of self. This is one of the most simple, beautiful love songs that I've heard in a long time. I'm moved to go inside and play this song along with, "When You Really Love Someone."

Alicia Keys is a brilliant young lady with an old soul, filled with wisdom and insight. "When You Really Love Someone" starts with, "I am a woman Lord knows I am" and what better way to express yourself than to lay claim to your essence?

There is beauty in my bones.

Photo Gallery

Photo 1 Author, Congo Square, New Orleans LA

Photo 2 Author, Congo Square, New Orleans LA

Photo 3 Author, cousins' reunion, Michigan City, IN

Photo 4 Author, MLK Memorial, Washington DC

173

Photo 5 Author, granddaughter and cousin, Central High School, Little Rock AR

Photo 5a Author, granddaughter and cousin, Central High School, Little Rock AR

Photo 6 Author, sons and nephew, Topeka KS

Photo 7 Aunt Bell, Nashville TN

Photo 8 Aunt Gloria Gypsy Mae, Michigan City IN

Photo 9 Author, Little Rock AR

Photo 9a Author, granddaughter, Little Rock AR

Photo 10 Cousin Clara Mae, Michigan City, IN

Photo 10a Aunt Doretha Mae, Greenwood, MS

Photo 11 Cousin Velma Mae, Sheboygan WI

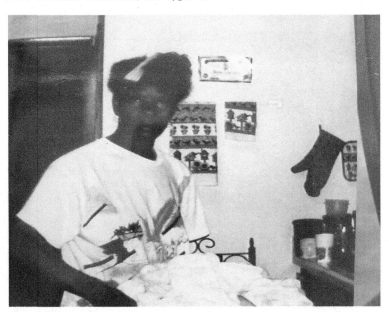

Photo 11a Cousin Velma Mae, Sheboygan WI

Photo 12 Author, granddaughter, Congo Square, New Orleans LA

Photo 12a Author, Congo Square, New Orleans LA

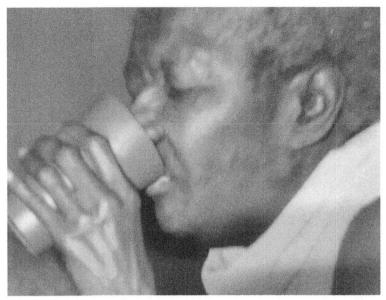

Photo 13 Aunt Willa Mae, Michigan City, IN

Photo 14 Author and friends

Photo 15 Author and sons, Miami, Oklahoma

*Photo 16 Author and sons, **Miami, Oklahoma***

Life Lessons

There was nothing easy about my life. Times were hard, but I survived. Looking back, I know that the things that happened to me have served me in ways I've only just begun to realize.

The short stories on the next few pages are snippets from another book I'm working on. I put them here as a way to pay homage to Yaya and all of those who lended a hand to my development.

I want her to know that her baby girl made it.

Because of Yaya, I'm strong. I'm confident. I'm free.

I hope my story made you laugh from knowing, cry from feeling, and inspire you to live your best life.

Robin White aka *Sippiana*

Take life by storm!

Knowing

My direct bloodline, Velma Mae, Auntie Gloria Mae, Wilma Mae, Georgia Mae, Salina Mae, Little Jean, Great Aunties Minnie and Mary, and my beautiful Yaya Barbara Ree, taught me the following:

We often willfully embrace burdens that weigh us down. These burdens afford us numerous problems, the opportunity to create purpose, and the chance to will existence through a crisis of difficulty.

Too often we fall prey to self-victimization. The greatest challenge in life is *knowing*, while sitting in the spirit. The ability to pull singleness of self into a meaningful embrace and knowing the difference between being lonely and being alone.

Airline Blues
Washington, D.C. June 2002

We arrived at Dulles Airport in Washington D.C. nearly 30 minutes late. The bulk of us were running to our connecting flight, rudely bumping into travelers as if we were the only ones who mattered.

I arrived at the departing gate breathless, panting, and digging around in my bag for my ticket. I had my head down talking to the attendant when I heard a foreign voice.

"You don't worry, the plane is late, you be just fine."

My mind jumped to attention. This voice alone drew me out of my own selfish thoughts and took me someplace else called *paranoid racist*.

I was thinking, "Hell no, why in the hell do they have this Middle Eastern motherfucker at my gate?"

My face must have showed some type of disapproval, because he began to get nervous and continued to reassure me that everything was alright.

I reached back into the halls of my mind and told myself to let go of all that labeling, propaganda bullshit that had been impressed upon me the past year. I smiled at the gentleman and the relief in his eyes made me feel so ashamed.

"Thank you," I said politely. "It is nice to know that you are available to reassure us that we'll get to our place of destination tonight."

I went to the seating area and listened to my flight colleagues complain.

How many times have I been discriminated against because my dark skin is a sin? How many times have the full demeanor of others changed when they learned that I am not from Africa, but am just a plain 'ole African American?

I hate it when people treat me as if I'm invisible. I used to feel ashamed when people refused to sit next to me. Now, I look at the fools standing up, and smile at them.

One half hour later, we boarded one of the mosquito planes - the kind that *buzzzzzz* like a bee. We boarded and I was sitting up front when the flight attended began to make her announcements.

She welcomed us to the flight and stopped, looked directly at me and asked, "What flight are we on?"

I damn near jumped out the seat and said, "Hell, don't *you* know what flight we are on?"

"This is my first day," she said full of embarrassment.

I shook my head knowing that this was not a good sign.

The gentlemen across from me came to her rescue and told her the flight number.

After she did her spiel and sat down, we were sitting another 10 minutes before the Captain came on and announced to us that we would depart as soon as we get some gas for the plane.

A voice asked, "What the hell does he mean as soon as we get some gas? Does he mean that we don't have any gas in the plane and that we were about to take off?"

The voice belonged to me.

We sat there another twenty minutes, and then the Captain announced to us that we were having some mechanical problems and the mechanic was on the way.

I snapped my seat belt off.

"Open this door," I said in anger. "Let me the hell off this plane."

"You can't do that," she said to me, visibly upset.

I looked at her, bit my lips, hunched over in the small plane, batted my eyes, and slowly said, "Giiirrrlll."

She gracefully opened the door and let me out.

My head was resting in my hand when the same gate attendant announced loudly, "Everyone is exiting the plane."

All the passengers disembarked, came to the boarding area, and started talking. Some told me that I had the right idea to get off the plane because that plane had been grounded. We were put on another plane.

Two weeks later, I was in Dulles airport again, waiting for my 5:30 flight to Phoenix, AZ. 5:45 came and went. At 6:00, I approached the ticket personnel. I kindly inquired about the plane's late arrival.

It's not like there's a traffic jam in the sky.

In my mind, I could see no reason for the delay. I already had a dislike for United Airlines due to their diligence for being late.

Finally, the ticket personnel announced the plane was delayed due to inclement weather. I called the DOI airline agent Omega to request another flight and was placed on American Airlines.

I told the ticket personnel from United and she got a little hot under the collar.

"You can't do that," she said.

"Young lady," I began. "Look at me and listen to my voice. I am extremely tired and really want to go home. Do you realize that once I get to Phoenix, I still have a four-hour drive ahead of me? Do you think I give a hoot about what you *think* I can't do?"

She stood and looked at me with a blank expression.

"I need for you to take care of the necessary paperwork so the computer crier (announcer) will let those bag people know where my luggage should go, and I need this before next year."

When I arrived at the American Airline gate, there were several passengers from the United Airlines gate already in line.

As I moved toward the ticket agent, I was picked out of line for a search.

I looked at the little man with the search stick and said, "Oh no, hell no. Y'all gonna make me lose my mind."

Everybody started laughing, including the stick man.

I threw up my arms and said, "Search me until your heart's content, but then please get me home."

What does this have to do with Beauty in My Bones you might ask?

Well, we all come from someplace and are trying to reach our destiny, be it a better job, relationship, emotional recovery, self-discovery, or just recognizing people's individuality through humanity or faith activism.

As we journey on faith, we tend to not only network and meet people, but we meet ourselves. We find the strength and courage to share our narrative as we explore and experience the love and courage of people all over the world.

Despite how society prescribes us, or how we are taught to perceive each other in unhealthy ways, there is magic in each of us and we are born with Beauty in Our Bones. It is in our DNA.

Also, we need a fart detector on airplanes.

People think somehow if it's a silent fart it doesn't smell. They are so wrong. I'm so damn tired of smelling other people's body functions on airplanes. I swear if a fart alert alarm went off on airplanes, people would watch what they eat, and they wouldn't be so quick to let loose on the plane thinking that it's undetected.

Banned from Dunkin Donuts

Boston May 2003

I love the water and for nearly two months, I rode the ferry from the Navy Yard to the Boston Harbor. The ferry was similar to New Orleans, except it had a different vibe.

This particular day, I exited the ferry, embracing the refreshing breeze.

Every morning, I'm anxious to walk past this beautiful building and watch people come and go.

For two weeks, I watched the comings and goings of people from this particular building. I'm not sure if I was drawn to the building, the construction workers, suits, teenagers, or policemen.

As my curiosity got the better of me, I followed people into the building.

Imagine my surprise to discover it was just a Dunkin Donuts!

But it wasn't your typical location.

There were no pink signs, hanging donuts, or coffee cups on this incredible building with amazing architect.

There, I stood in line.

As my turn approached, I'd politely let people cut in front of me. The goal was not to buy Donuts, but instead kill time through people watching.

One of the employees was suspiciously watching me, so I departed.

However, I repeated the same routine for several days.

My date with Dunkin Donuts was quite enjoyable.

One particular day, I seemed to have irritated the store manager.

People were going about their day, ordering and eating, when this nasal thick voice inquired, "Ma'am, can I help you?"

He repeated himself before I realized the question was directed at me.

I boldly replied, "No."

In a loud Boston accent, he said, "Ma'am, you have been entering my store this past week and haven't bought anything. What can I help you with?"

People backed up to distance themselves from me as if I smelled.

Mr. Officer of the GD Law continued to sip his coffee, causally glancing in my direction.

The manager asked, "Who are you?"

Did he think I was some sort of spy sent to steal Dunkin Donuts secret recipes?

Simply stating my name was out of the question and my imagination swelled with delicious thoughts.

In a quiet soft-spoken voice, I clearly said, "I is a runaway slave, searching for a safe house on the Underground Railroad. I is running away from my 6 and 8 year old Massas. Those dang on chillin won't me to cook and clean all day. I took the mind to leave them be and become a fugitive slave."

You could literally hear cups hit the floor and liquid splash.

Officer of the GD Law and others were choking on their Donuts and Coffee.

It was a calmly silence, but then the stunned customers erupted into laughter.

The manager came from behind the counter with his twisted, confrontational, managerial face, turned to the officer of the GD Law, and said, "What are you going to do?"

The Officer with a perplexed look said, "What am I going to do? Arrest her for being a runaway slave? She ain't broke no laws?"

The manager told me to leave his store and never show my face around there again as he kindly escorted me out of the door.

This is how I was banned from Dunkin Donuts.

Dupont Circle
Washington D.C. March 2003

One of my favorite pastimes is to people watch.

There I was in DuPont Circle, walking towards this beautiful sister, and I must give it to her, she had a nice frame.

As the classic White Van rounded the corner a brother leaned out the window and gave the sister a shout out.

Now, I'm not saying what the brother was doing was right, but it seems that this type of behavior can be traced back to the beginning of time. I wondered if she was secretly amused, or if the frown on her face was disapproval of his behavior.

There is a time when we miss all the innocence of cat calling, especially when you often find yourself relocated and far away from all that is familiar. We often fail to realize how much we miss our culture or the small things that can irritate us, until it's absent and the void is undeniable.

Come walk with me and revisit Topeka, Kansas in 1996.

My colleagues and I were strolling up Topeka Street on a food quest. Now, mind you, downtown Topeka is heavily populated with banks, businesses, restaurants, and packed with people of distinct non-color.

As we walked towards this young man, I noticed he began to slow down, staring as if he knew me. He looked me square in my eyes and smiled.

I responded to his smile with a smile. As we walked past this young man, he said, "Oh, My Lord," and fell to his knees clasping his hands. "Oh, my God, I thank God, I thank your mother and I thank you sista for that onion. What a beautiful sight. Your onion just brings tears to my eyes."

I had no idea what the hell he was talking about. I stood there, looking stupid, thinking, "do I smell like an onion?" until he said, "I could walk behind you forever. You were made for my gaze."

Unbelievable. Slowly, it dawned on me that he was loudly talking about my backside!

Professional men in suits were walking past with their heads down, but their eyes were looking. I knew they overheard; their hesitant smiles said it all.

The nosey ass women stood still to take in the whole scene.

I really didn't know how to feel.

I looked at the brother and found a new appreciation for him.

This was my world.

I have arrived from Albuquerque, New Mexico safely home.

This man, in all his innocence, would do nothing to hurt me. A damn burst from within and I threw my head back and laughed.

This was the best laugh I had in a long time.

The Creator has a great sense of humor. He sent this young man my way to brighten my day. He not only validated me in the craziest way, but he did it with a sense of humor, and it did my heart some good.

After living in several parts of the country and in areas lacking people of color, I found that I missed my brothers on the corner.

I missed brothers saying, "Do fries come with that shake? Call 911, my heart was just stolen. I love your sway; your sweet sashay drives me crazy. Don't go. Don't you know that you are creating a disturbance in my mind?"

My mind returned to DuPont Circle.

The sister's body was banging.

Maybe her frown was over the displeasure to the tight-fitting shoes she was sporting. Her feet seemed a bit squished as stockings smothered her flesh pouring out of the shoes seeking amnesty.

People of Today
Chicago, Illinois, September 1989

People are good at being deaf and blind when it serves a convenience for them.

Times have changed; most people will look the other way quickly before they make an effort to help you. Especially if you are in danger.

This was a glorious, warm, yet breezy morning and I boarded the Amtrak headed to Chicago, Illinois Union Station. While walking down State Street in Chicago, I heard some commotion going on behind me. Assuming the noise was just loud conversation, I paid it no mind.

As I neared a stoplight, I was suddenly grabbed from behind and lifted in the air. This man walked from the corner, and while walking, somehow managed to turn me around to face him. He put me down and, pinning me against the wall, he leaned in and asked me for my phone number.

I was literally squirming and in shock, the situation not not fully registering.

Cars were at the stoplight. We were so close to those vehicles; the drivers could hear our conversation.

I was in my late 20s and weighed 120 pounds. My heart was racing fast. I was pushing the man and not one driver came to my rescue. If someone had just said, "Miss, are you alright?" the man would've turned to them, which probably would have afforded me an opportunity to run.

But no, this was the day when all the drivers wanted to be on their best behavior and not interfere or appear to be nosey. So, they choose to ignore the scene of this woman with a frantic look on her face, struggling with a man.

The kicker was, a street musician was sitting there as the man decided to lift me up in the air again. The street musician was cleaning his saxophone slowly and humming, as if he was watching television.

I stopped squirming and relaxed as he gently lowered me to the ground and again said, "Baby, I want your phone number."

Dumbfounded, I stuttered, "I-I don't-don't live here."

"I don't care where you live," he said. "I want your phone number."

I graciously rattled off something.

He smiled, "Give me that number again."

I gave him the same number.

Satisfied, he nodded and said, "I will be calling you, sister. Gotta get to work."

He finally left and disappeared around the corner.

My body was so tense and my feet refused to move. I loudly exhaled and released the tension. I collapsed against the wall for support.

Just then the fool came back around the corner and said, "Baby, what's your name?"

To this day, I don't know what I said, but he was satisfied and again, walked away.

From that day to this one, when I travel, I have no problem with scratching in unmentionable places, talking to imaginary friends, and even answering if I need to.

People will stay the hell out of my way. Especially when I argue with my imaginary adversaries.

I am assured no one will be accosting me for anything, not even directions.

Stand by Your Man

My schooling of "stand by your man" is reinforced because it is a little different. As a child, I watched the meaning of "stand by your man."

As I witness the political fallout from politicians caught with their hands in the cookie jar, I can't wrap my mind around how their wives dutifully claim their dedication and devotion to *stand by their man.*

I recall at one point; our home was pretty empty. My older siblings were always visiting Grandma Lilbit in Schlater , Mississippi at the McMillen Plantation. My younger siblings were quiet (unless I stirred up something). They were just good siblings, none-adventurous at all. As the rebel rouser, I caused them to get in trouble a lot.

Don't get me wrong, they grew into their own personalities and caused enough trouble for an army.

I came home from school one day to find this little caramel colored girl with red hair like me. Instantly, she was named Dirty Red, as I was Little Red. Although we talked, she clung to my

Yaya. I instantly assumed she was a family member sent ahead like so many others and was missing her family. So, instead of being jealous, I let her have Yaya, knowing it was only temporarily.

Three weeks later, Dirty Red was gone, and it was during Yaya and my's downtime that I learned the truth.

"All women have is each other, Lil' Red," Yaya said. "One day, you will understand what I'm talking about."

I nodded my head, convinced she was right.

"Women are supposed to support each other. We are the backbone of the community," she insisted. "Little Red, when you grow up and I hear about you fighting a woman over a man, it is going to be hell to pay the captain!"

As it turns out, Dirty Red was my father's child. Her mother took sick and needed someone to care for her daughter. Yaya knew about Baba's other children. She said she didn't blame the women, nor was she angry at them. She took care of Dirty Red until her mother recovered from her illness.

I was taught the concept of dignity, integrity, and compromise early on. In any relationship (family, mate, or friend), how much of yourself are you willing to give and/or sacrifice?

The women in the family gifted me many life lessons. Two of their womanly gifts remain with me to this day:

One: Don't ever compete with, or fight, another woman over a man.

Two: Never, ever try to compete with drugs.

Women, in particular women of color, are born on the battlefield. We have to fight for respect throughout our lives, be it while pursuing an education, in the workplace, or, sadly, in our own homes.

A woman should never feel threated or have to fight within the sanctuary of her home.

The one place a woman should be secured is in her dwellings. It is her man's place to protect her at all times. He should not bring trouble to your doorstep. If another woman should accost you about your man, don't spill your anger on her. Take it up with your man.

Women should always stick together.

This is an echo from the past and it is always in my head.

Admittedly, such a code of honor isn't always applicable, as both women and men must be conscious of the rules of engagement.

Due to my small stature, there were times a few sisters came at me sideways and, with an apology, I would *git with the gitting* and peel their heads off.

The Day Is Dawn
Boston, Massachusetts May 2003

People were walking down State Street in Boston Massachusetts at breakneck speed. Most had their heads down, purposely not making eye contact. Other pedestrians swiftly walked alongside the curb of the sidewalk.

Suddenly, right in front of me, moving ever so slowly, was this huge woman.

She was shaped like a real beehive and lacked color, as if she'd never seen the sun. She was pale like a chicken before frying.

"Creator," I asked silently. "Please remove any stupid thoughts from my head and hold my tongue."

As I got closer to the beehive lady, I could hear her laboring to breathe. He mini skirt, which wasn't covering very much, probably wasn't a miniskirt at all.

Her legs and arms were shaped like ham shanks and her poor shoes (high heels, no less) were turned over every which way and seemed to scream, "MERCY!"

Her face was colored very sad, and although her eyes were clear and peaceful blue, they were troubled as she, also, attempted to avoid any eye contact. She walked with her head down as if in search of something.

The smirks, giggles, and rude remarks from the 9 to 5 (supposedly professional suits) failed to give her any slack.

Somehow, my feet managed to put me directly in her path and she had to look up.

In those sad eyes, I saw a pillar of strength and courage.

I saw the beauty in her bones.

She had on too much makeup, like Tammy Faye Baker. Her long, fake eyelashes looked like spider legs. Her scarlet red lipstick was pretty thick, and her cheeks were colored in the same red, causing her to look like Raggedy Ann. Her foundation didn't match her pale skin. It was almost like meeting Ms. Piggy in person.

Her presence said, "Accept me as I am."

It stirred my friend compassion and the smile that warmed my lips was genuine.

This loud voice said, "Keep on doing you. Be bold and beautiful. Big girls are amazing."

She melted like chocolate kissed by the sun.

She smiled back and, oh, my goodness, she had the most stunning smile. Her perfect, white teeth were striking. You could tell that the smile spread to her heart as tears swelled in her eyes. She was gorgeous and her walk took on a new meaning.

With newfound strength, she moved with a purpose.

I literally felt her presence shift.

Something happened in that moment and it was good.

Maybe she, too, saw the beauty in her bones.

You & Me
Little Rock, Arkansas September 2020

We are faced with generational trauma, initiating a moral emergent to address this unending cycle of our unheard voices. We have been invisible as a people for centuries, we are conditioned to fear, and our presence is a threat as we constantly meet aggression.

My soul is strained with images of brutality suffered upon all men and women of color. We are part of a long-standing lineage that have endured unmeasurable injustice.

My Sons, Brothers, Sisters, and Fathers you pour out of my pores grasping for life, filled with indignation, smoldering, seeking refuge from the slowly dragging bowels of hell only to enter a world cruel to you and me. We are born into a society fated in racial jackets.

Yet, I am accused of barbaric ways, while introduced to horrifying acts of violence, trickery, lies and deception. We are constantly imprisoned as we revisit, re-live, and re-experience an eternity of pain and brutality, And we are supposed to be pleased for the generosity of systemic discrimination enthralled in a nation of alleged compassion, liberty and freedom for all.

It is taxing, watching and re-living the norm of pain and brutality put upon you and me, deliberately stomping the goodness out of us. Yet, it cannot stick, because the beauty in me and you will outshine all the planted seeds of bad deeds.

The truth flows through our veins and it is our reign that will bring down the thunder because we are the people of a mighty nation. We are beautiful and strong. Remember there's beauty in our bones!

I don't know what else to say except, "Do you hear me? Do you see me!"

Afterthoughts

As a child during our traditional naming ceremony, I was given the name *Oyo Rinde,* which means *Joy Walks In.* As an adolescent, I was given the second name of *Oso Tunde,* which means *The Seer Comes Again.*

However, those who had their hand on me, blessed me and shared their universal knowledge with me. Although I was but a child, with no education, they taught me to see the world through a child's eye and heart and to serve for the greater of justice and universal truths. I was taught the concept of community servant (caring for others always) as a girlchild, and today, as I represent more than six generations, I stand in celebration of the human spirit.

Sippianna is a true calling to my nature as a product of Indiana, Mississippi, Louisiana, and South Carolina. It was in Lake Michigan, the woods, sandy beaches, Mississippi Magnolia trees, and red clay dirt where I not only picked cotton, but pecans too. South Carolina, the beautiful sea islands, are dark as midnight, filled with magic, strong family bonds, and rich dialect, and all are ripe with history and are in my DNA.

I was told that I didn't have to go to Africa because she traveled across the waters to me.

I am to remember always beyond those people into the communities who are witness to the making of me. *Sippianna* is simply a servant in God's favor. His hands upon me allowed me to explore, discover, and recover my very being. I transformed all their teachings into a servant leader.

I am the first of many things, the first to dare leave from around my family as an adult, and the first to complete college (since then, many more family members are doing and have done so).

Self-Validation is my greatest motivation, and my elders were continuously validating me with Anna, being our purpose a purpose, In God's Favor, the artist to transform the impossible to possible in light, love, and beauty. I am hereby crowned *Sippianna,* the servant leader.

I was blessed, yep, unseen, unwanted, and unheard, out of eight siblings, I rebelled against mainstream society. Compelled to run from family secrets, I fell into the arms, mind, and heart of my elders all across the North and South. I had no misgivings because, with each lesson, love was adorned. Most importantly, they taught me that I am a child of the universe. And with that, it does not matter where I go or belong, I am responsible for those communities.

Iris, you stimulate me and those re-memories. Although some thoughts/reflections were purposely shut down, it is easier to revisit with someone trustworthy by my side. As we continue the dialogue, I feel great about the start, because I can see beauty in its making.

Ase'

About the Author

Growing up (unfortunate) and orphaned at a young age, life for Robin White was anything but ideal, the abuse she and her siblings suffered at the hands of an older sibling, threatened to derail the author's destiny..

It was the solid foundation planted by her Yaya and (numerous female relatives) that sustained her through difficult times as a child and the challenges on the road to adulthood.

The lessons of Yaya centered around the premise of observing, being still, and hearing the soft quiet voice within , even when the world around her was raging.

Although Yaya (departed) much too soon, she left behind a wealth of strength and a tapestry of integrity, conditional love and purpose.

Robin White's GullaGeechee and Creole backgrounds present an unusual voice that is not easily accepted by the mainstream.

Some contributing factors may include the fact that Robin was uprooted and displayed multiple times during her youth Robin ran away from a Detention Center at age thirteen and became a migrant picking oranges and grapefruit at the age of fourteen. Dubbed by her elders as Sippianna, White contributes her universal concepts to roots that stemmed from a southern heritage (Mississippi, South Carolina, and Louisiana).

White worked with rival gangs in Gary, Indiana and partnered with the Chicago Department of Human Services gang intervention network under the late Mayor Harold Washington regime. She worked with the Southern Ute in Ignacio, Colorado, developing cultural curricula to increase cultural pride and empowerment.

Under the auspice of NAACP, White was the co-founder of *Rites of Passage*, a gang prevention and intervention program. The program was established in 1992 and still exists today in Albuquerque, New Mexico. She established the Campbell & White Consulting, providing expertise to local law enforcement agencies, youth service organizations, and the Five Sandoval Indian Pueblo on subjects such as youth empowerment, principles of nonviolence, mobilizing the community, cultural competence, and servant leadership.

In addition to her autobiographical writing, Robin is also working on three other works; Subjugation of My Pigmentation, a call and response collaborative collection of poems, and a collection of short stories she is working on with her incarcerated nephew. Love Letters to A Black Man, and an academia work titled A Bridge Between Two World, a Graduate school thesis that turned into manuscript upon the urging of several instructors, the universal concept revolves around best practices of servant leadership and civic discourse.

Although she dropped out of school in the ninth grade, Robin went on to earn a Bachelor's of Science in Criminal Justice at Indiana University Northwest and a masters in leadership, Social Issues and Public Policy from the Union Institute & University.

A native of Michigan City, Indiana, the educator, humanitarian, faith activist, and community civic activist currently resides in Little Rock, Arkansas. Her hobbies include cross country skiing, art collecting, and writing. She self-published her first book, *Reports from the Soul*, which is a collection of short stories and poems.

the **Butterfly Typeface**

"We Make Good Great"

www.butterflytypeface.com

Made in the USA
Coppell, TX
03 March 2023

13667292R10125